# HELL
# and
# HEAVY WATER

A Glace Bay Heavy Water Plant Story

By

Roland MacInnis

## DEDICATION

This book is dedicated to the memory of many dear friends in the Canadian heavy water industry who lived this story in their own way and in their own time.

## ACKNOWLEDGEMENTS

I am grateful for the help of friends in the Canadian heavy water industry who offered their first-hand knowledge. A sincere thank you to Tim Andreeff, Carl Taylor, Denis Bouvette, Gerry Armitage, Bob Sissingh, Betty Rankin and Frank Kober for their contributions to this story. A special thanks to my wife, Judy, who, as editor and advisor, contributed immeasurably to this book. Thanks also to Ray Renton, Rob Swetnam, Anita Rose, Shirley MacPherson, Bill and Norma Adams, Bob McKay, George Evans, Keith Greig, Joan Corbett, for their interest and support.

## NOTES

I've simplified some explanations for the benefit of the general reader. I've edited some stories provided by others or derived from books and other sources, e.g. Wikipedia. My purpose in doing so is not to misrepresent real events but to present a better story. Events are presented from the point of view of the author and from other contributors, as acknowledged. The passage of time and faulty memory may have led to some errors or omissions. If so, these mistakes are unintentional and are the responsibility of the author. Notwithstanding the many challenges, most employees of the plant, including me, felt that it was a great place to work. As Carl Taylor recently said, "I think there are many people who feel that their best job in life was taken away from them."

## CONTENTS

5

# SYNOPSIS

This is a story about Canada's first large scale heavy water plant. It is based on the recollections of people who worked at the plant or were otherwise associated with Canada's heavy water industry. The story includes information gleaned from publicly available sources. This book is not per se a 'history' in the academic sense...it is a 'mostly true' story.

The plant was announced in 1963, closed in 1985, and fifty years later, in 2013, it was plowed under and largely forgotten.

From its beginning it was a troubled plant. It took three attempts and persistent political, financial and technical commitment to bring it to full production. By that time, the early 1980s, Canada was awash in heavy water.

The plant hugged the rocky shores of the cold North Atlantic. It existed a hundred miles and a hundred years past the ill-fated HMS Titanic, now rusting on the ocean bottom. It bordered the undersea coalmines of Cape Breton Island, in the town of Glace Bay.

For some, the term 'heavy water' conjures thoughts of a WW2 raid in Telemark, Norway, the Manhattan Project, Chalk River, Ontario, the atomic bomb, Hiroshima, Albert Einstein, Enrico Fermi and J. Robert Oppenheimer. For others, it means electricity. For the anti-nuclear people, it means unacceptable risk, however small.

After WW2, Canada experienced spectacular economic growth. Every region of the country struggled to supply energy to expanding industries in mining, metals and manufacturing. In response, Atomic Energy of Canada Limited, AECL, developed its CANDU, [Canada Deuterium Uranium], nuclear-electric power system. Heavy water is a vital component of the CANDU system because it enables nuclear fission. No heavy water, no CANDU!

By the early 1960s, the Canadian Province of Ontario had exploited its major hydro resources, e.g., Niagara Falls. However, blessed with ample deposits of uranium but lacking coal, oil, and natural gas, Ontario placed a big bet on CANDU as its main source of electricity[1] . New Brunswick

---

[1] In 2017, CANDU nuclear power was 35 percent of Ontario's electrical energy capacity and contributed 63 percent of the energy produced.

Power and Quebec Hydro also committed to CANDU, although to a lesser extent.

Ontario's commitment to AECL's CANDU system created a demand for heavy water. A looming heavy water shortage became the potential 'Achilles heel'[2] of the CANDU system

In August 1963, the Cape Breton Post announced, '... *the biggest industrial complex in Cape Breton since the turn-of-the-century."* There was much local excitement about a heavy water plant, an atomic-age industry with hundreds of good-paying jobs. For a hardscrabble region with persistent unemployment and a worrisome dependence on failing coal and steel industries this was salvation itself.

The Cape Breton Post's optimistic words heralded Canada's re-entry into large-scale heavy water production[3]

The original plant was the brainchild of American scientist-inventor and self-professed businessman, Jerome Spevack, President of Deuterium of Canada Limited, [DCL].

Plant construction was plagued with labour problems, strikes and walkouts, that gave Cape Breton's labour force a black eye. Once built and commissioned, DCL struggled to get this uniquely designed plant to work.

In his 1991 paper, "Canada's Heavy Water Story," Howard K. Rae, Vice President of AECL, said,

*"In selecting the first heavy water supplier, AECL did not give sufficient weight to experience in managing large projects or operating chemical plants, the government could and did play an overriding role in*

---

[2] Achilles heel means area of weakness, vulnerable spot. According to the Greek Myth, when Achilles was a baby, it was foretold that he would die young. His mother took him to a river that was supposed to offer powers of invulnerability. She dipped his body into the water; however, the water of the magical river did not wash his heel. Achilles grew up to be a man of war who survived many great battles. One day, a poisonous arrow shot at him was lodged in his heel, killing him shortly afterwards.

[3] During WW2 Canada produced a small amount of heavy water from a COMINCO plant in Trail, BC.

*decisions...These two factors combined with an unhappy choice of
Deuterium of Canada Limited to build the first plant."[4]*

By 1970, following investment of about $100 million, the plant failed
spectacularly. It had a 'real' operating life of about twelve days and was by
any measure a technical, financial and political disaster.

Plant failure precipitated a crisis in heavy water supply for Ontario's
newly built CANDU power reactors. Commissioning problems at the
second Cape Breton heavy water plant, in Port Hawkesbury added to
Canada's heavy water worries.

As a stopgap measure, Canada bought heavy water from the US,
Russia, Sweden and other countries, sometimes in small amounts at
inflated prices. Unfortunately, the worldwide supply of heavy water was
limited and insufficient in the long run. A reliable domestic supply of
heavy water was vital.

In response to Cape Breton heavy water plant problems, AECL
committed to constructing a plant in Bruce County, Ontario, site of
Ontario Hydro's first 'commercial' 200 MW CANDU power reactor. In
mid-1973, following some teething problems, the Bruce Heavy Water
Plant, BHWP, was on its way to resounding production success.

The failure of the DCL plant threatened the political fortunes of Nova
Scotia's Government led by Premier George Isaac Smith, successor to
Nova Scotia political icon, Robert L. Stanfield. Smith had little choice but
to assume ownership of the ill-fated plant and had to swallow a multi-
million-dollar payoff to Spevack.

By the mid 1970s, thanks to the political clout of Cape Breton MP,
Hon. Alan J. McEachen, the plant, like the proverbial cat, got another
lease on life.

By the early 1980s, the now-rehabilitated plant, owned and operated
by AECL, produced hundreds of tons of heavy water. Alas! Production
success was thirteen years late.

Thanks to the robust science and technology research program at
AECL's Chalk River Labs, led by Howard Rae, Canada had mastered

[4] Rae, H. K., "Canada's Heavy Water Story", Chemical Engineering in
Canada - An Historical Perspective, Edited by L. W. Shemilt, Canadian
Society for Chemical Engineering, p. 334, 1991.

heavy water production and the country was drowning in heavy water. The Bruce Heavy Water Plant, alone, had a production capacity approaching 1000 tons per year.

The 1985 budget of the newly-elected Government of Brian Mulroney closed Cape Breton's heavy water plants with the loss of hundreds of jobs.

The plants were eventually dismantled, and the gigantic steel towers were explosively toppled, felled like giant redwoods, and sold for scrap.

The Glace Bay plant story did not end there. The plant played a small part in a Nobel Prize winning discovery by a son of Cape Breton.

In a hard rock mine in Sudbury, Ontario, 7000 feet down, surplus heavy water awaited yet another important role. In 2015, Arthur McDonald, born and raised in Sydney, Cape Breton, was awarded the Nobel Prize in Physics for his work with neutrinos, a fundamental subatomic particle[5]. He proved that neutrinos have mass. This discovery changed the understanding of the innermost workings of matter. Some of his experiments were conducted at SNOLAB, the Neutrino Observatory in Sudbury, Ontario.[6] His prize-winning experiments used Canada's surplus heavy water, including heavy water produced at the Glace Bay plant.

---

[5] Neutrinos are a subatomic particle that permeate space. Thousands of neutrinos pass through your body every second of every day.

[6] SNOLAB is a Canadian physics laboratory, underground, at a depth of two km, located in a Sudbury, Ontario nickel mine.

# PROLOGUE

Once upon a time, a large plant grew along the rocky shores of the Atlantic Ocean. It wasn't leafy, green or edible. It was big and shiny, sometimes stinky, and produced a rare chemical called deuterium oxide, better known as heavy water.

Picture this: several big shiny towers, two-hundred feet high, 50 feet wide, a 400-foot flare stack sticking straight up, a giant barber pole, a scattering of other large shiny vessels and tanks, large and small pipes running everywhere, bending, looping. Hundreds of tons of toxic gas, H2S, under high pressure, wanting always to escape. Thousands of gallons of bubble-burdened water pulsing through the plant's innards, every hour, every day, 365 days a year. High-pressure steam hissing from a decrepit coal-fired power plant, whizzing through hot steel pipes, feeding a $300 million pressure cooker. The control room: wall-to-wall instruments, buttons, dials and charts. Control room operators: hovering, watching, sometimes relaxing, always ready to react to strange sounds, alarms, flashing lights, a thump, a bump a clang. Behind a chain link perimeter fence: a few large buildings and many smaller ones, a guardhouse with uniformed guards bordering a large parking lot. Sounds: disembodied voices, issuing from pole-mounted PA speakers. People: on the move, purposeful, hard-hatted, work-booted, coverall-clothed, safety protected.

It has been more than thirty years since the Glace Bay Heavy Water Plant, [GBHWP], ceased production. More than sixty years since the idea of indigenous heavy water production influenced the decisions of Canada's nuclear pioneers. That's a long time to wait before scratching away at the hard crust of memory.

This story is about the events that shaped the plants future as told by some of the people who worked there. Employees and contractors came from all provinces of Canada and several other countries. Most were born and raised on Cape Breton Island.

This is an inside story and not a history per se. It is not a primer on how to manufacture heavy water. It is written for employees, families and friends and the 'just plain curious'. The story has been created from the author's personal recollections and a few first-person accounts from others. There may also be a bit of hearsay in the story.

It's a story of struggle: beginning with colossal failure, recovery, redemption, and finally, in the way that many Cape Breton industries have ended their lives, caught in a trap of change.

The plant 'lived' in one form or other for about 20 years and gave rise to many stories, not all of which are true, remembered or written here.

Heavy water production is difficult. GBHWP employees faced many challenges in learning how to do it well. Help in overcoming obstacles came in many guises. The studies of research scientists, knowledge shared by other plants, clever engineers, smart women, they all helped the plant to survive and, eventually, succeed. Most challenges arose from the usual sources, the needs of powerful people, the perversity of inanimate objects and the mysteries of the universe.

The late Hon. Allan Joseph McEachen, perhaps the most influential Cape Breton politician in recent history, was an important member of Canada's Parliament. In his day, he played a key role in all things affecting Cape Breton. He influenced the decision to locate heavy water plants in Cape Breton. With a history of 'bumping and jiggling' Cape Breton's economic pin-ball machine, 'Allan J.' set the GBHWP story in motion. His successor, Hon. David Dingwall played his part in the latter years of the plant.

Canadian Government Agencies, particularly the Atomic Energy Control Board, [AECB], worried about heavy water plants and it took them a while to learn how to regulate them. The hazard posed by these plants was not taken lightly.

This story is mostly anecdotal and, as in the movies, a few stories have been 'improved' for dramatic purposes. Occasionally, money, politicians and governments colour this story.

Like ancient Carthage, the plant was razed to bare ground and a few half-buried concrete tombstones bear mute witness to a long-forgotten story…once upon a time.

# THIRST FOR HEAVY WATER

In the 1940s American atomic bombs exploded in the Pacific. The United States launched an "Atoms for Peace" program in 1953 and every major industrialized country sought atomic energy's promised peaceful benefits. Production of electricity topped the list. Canada was well positioned to develop a nuclear-electric power system.

The creation of Atomic Energy of Canada Limited, [AECL] in 1952 and its subsequent partnership with Ontario Hydro led to development and deployment of the CANDU, [Canada Deuterium Uranium], power reactor.

By the mid-1950s, AECL and Ontario Hydro had built power demonstration units. By 1962, Canadian heavy water production was deemed essential to the success of the CANDU program[7].

In 1963, AECL received approval from the federal government to seek bids for the supply of 900 tons[8] of heavy water over a five-year period at about $20 per pound.

AECL favoured Alberta for heavy water production because of cheap natural gas and experienced chemical plant operators like Imperial Oil.

Jerome S. Spevack, President of Deuterium Canada Limited, DCL, submitted a heavy water supply bid and he proposed to build a plant in Alberta.

Nova Scotia's Industrial Estates Ltd. also wanted the plant and they promised millions of dollars in government financing.

Sniffing the political winds, Spevack changed his proposed plant location from Alberta to Cape Breton.

Lorne Gray, President of AECL, had grave concerns about DCL's capability but his political masters viewed the DCL plant as an opportunity for regional economic development in an otherwise undeveloped region of the country.

Over Gray's strong objections, the federal government instructed AECL to award a heavy water supply contract to DCL. From 1955 to 1978

---

[7] H.K. Rae, Canada's Heavy Water Story, Chemical Engineering in Canada, 1991, Canadian Society for Chemical Engineering.

[8] Canada committed to the metric system in the 1970s. One ton is roughly equivalent to one Mg., [one million grams or one Megagram].

approximately 20,000 MW of CANDU generated power was committed and the projected demand for Canadian sourced heavy water skyrocketed[9].

---

[9] For the CANDU systems of that era, each MW requires a Mg [or one ton] of heavy water. Thus 20,000 tons of heavy water.

# BIG NEWS

The weather was miserable in Sydney Nova Scotia on Saturday, August 31, 1963. The temperature never got above 17°C. Soupy fog reduced visibility and a cold drizzle spattered the wrap-around windshields of the tail-finned Chevrolets sold by local car dealer, R. J. Logue. Notwithstanding the gloomy weather, the editor of the local paper, the Cape Breton Post, described in sunny terms ..."the biggest industrial complex in Cape Breton since the turn of the century...the biggest undertaking here since construction of the steel plant."

Details of a $50 million heavy water plant, to be constructed some 17 miles from Sydney, were apparently completed after top-secret negotiations that stretched over eight months. He outlined a multimillion-dollar investment by the provincial government through its investment agency, Industrial Estates Limited. The article said construction of the new plant would create opportunities for local coal mines and pave the way, for a score of allied industries. The demand for large quantities of heavy water for CANDU power reactors drove the need for production in Canada, Ontario Hydro's multibillion-dollar commitment to CANDU-produced electricity.

And so, on this wet August day, the people of Cape Breton learned of plans to build the first heavy water plant in Canada since the 1943 construction of a small plant in Trail, British Columbia[10].

On December 4, 1963, three months later, another miserable day, cloudy with rain, fog and snow. The Post described "glowing prospects" for a $30 million heavy water plant. The plant would be located near Glace Bay. The article was laced with superlatives, "a world centre for research and development in the nuclear age... the most modern project for nuclear creation." It went on to say that the plant would, make Glace Bay one of the most modern places on earth. It praised Robert Stanfield, then Premier of Nova Scotia, and encouraged readers to re-elect his government. News reports thereafter discussed construction progress and

---

[10] The Trail plant was built by Cominco and financed by the United States War Department under the direction of the Manhattan Project. It shut down in 1945, replaced by newer US-based heavy water plants with lower production costs.

forecast that first heavy water production would occur in 1966. As forecasts go, it rivalled Mayor Drapeau's somewhat famous forecast that the 1976 Montreal Olympics, "Can no more have a deficit, than a man can have a baby." It took until 2006 before Quebecers finally paid off the $1.5 billion debt.

# SPEVACKED

*"Double, double toil and trouble;*
*fire burn and cauldron bubble."*
*- Shakespeare, Macbeth: IV*

Jerome Spevack, American scientist, inventor and engineer, patented a process to produce heavy water. Later on, he sued the US government for infringement of this patent.

DuPont engineers at the USAEC's Savannah River Plant, [SRP], had much to offer DCL and its contractors by way of practical advice on heavy water production. However, Spevack's lawsuit discouraged any exchange of information from SRP to DCL. Spevack decided to go it alone and he chose Burns and Roe Inc. to perform detailed engineering and Brown and Root, Canada Limited, to undertake construction.

Brown and Root's, US parent was a Texas company with an interesting history. In the early days of the company they developed strong political connections to Lyndon B. Johnson, a Texas Congressman, who became President of the United States in 1963 following the Dallas Texas assassination of John F. Kennedy.

Halliburton Energy Services eventually acquired Brown and Root. Former US Vice President, Dick Cheney served as chairman and CEO of Halliburton prior to his election as Vice-President along with President, George W. Bush, a former Texas Governor. Halliburton was awarded contracts for services to the US military during the war in Iraq during the time of the Bush/Cheney administration.

# COME FROM AWAY

In the mid 1960s, Atomic Energy of Canada Limited, AECL, and Ontario Hydro fully committed to the CANDU system. The province of Ontario, facing the limitations of hydro power, lacked fossil fuels but had abundant uranium deposits. Thus, nuclear power made sense.

Because of its role in the development of nuclear technology in World War II, Canada had a capable scientific and technical foundation. Development of large-scale nuclear-electric power system required hundreds more highly skilled people and Canada recruited, trained, and deployed a CANDU army.

Few countries possessed large numbers of people with skills and experience in nuclear power. Fortunately, the United Kingdom was well advanced in its development of nuclear power and had many highly skilled people ready willing and able to emigrate.

Hitler's threat to England in the early stages of WW2 necessitated relocation of some of England's top nuclear physicists to Chalk River, Ontario. Thus, Canada had a vital channel of nuclear power expertise.

# DOUBLE TROUBLE

Towards the end of 1964 the federal government 'doubled down' and instructed AECL to offer yet another contract to DCL. This time, DCL was asked to double Glace Bay plant capacity. DCL and the Province of Nova Scotia agreed to share costs equally.

Frequent strikes delayed the project, drained DCL's coffers, and gave Nova Scotia workers a black eye. Such problems foreshadowed the difficult road ahead.

Mired in construction delays and cash flow problems, DCL accepted the challenge.

DCL's financial problems deepened and the province was soon forced to assume a controlling interest in the company. Spevack was retained as President of DCL. Spevack's continuing role raised the ire of Gerald Regan, Leader of the Official Opposition in the N.S. Legislature.

# TWELVE DAYS

Jerome Spevack understood the theoretical basis of heavy water production but neither he nor DCL had previously designed, constructed or operated a heavy water plant. Spevack's plant operated in theory but not, as it turned out, in the nuts and bolts of practice.

The choice of Atlantic Ocean salt water as the source of heavy water turned out to be a huge mistake. Salt water contains slightly more deuterium than fresh water, but the difference is trivial. Most importantly, salt water is notoriously corrosive as every operator of steel-hulled ships can attest. Billions of dollars have been spent by the world's navies to combat the corrosive effects of salt water.

H2S is an essential ingredient in the heavy water 'recipe' but it poses a double-barrelled threat. It is a safety hazard because when mixed with hot salt water it corrodes steel.

In 1968, with one unit of the DCL plant complete, start-up failed. Design, materials and process problems bedevilled subsequent start-up attempts.

During one of these attempts a cloud of poisonous hydrogen sulphide gas escaped[11]. Fortunately prevailing winds blew the gas out to sea away from the plant and the town.

In 1969 a second start-up was attempted but because the combination of salt water with hydrogen sulphide it resulted in a catastrophic equipment failure.

The DCL plant had an operating life of 12 days, and to the disappointment of everyone involved, Government, investors, employees, citizens, taxpayers, it failed to produce any heavy water.

The Atomic Energy Control Board[12], revoked the plant's operating license.

---

[11] H2S is highly toxic. A concentration of seven hundred parts-per-million, of H2S in air is lethal. A large release would threaten the lives of people living nearby.

[12] The Atomic Energy Control Board is an agency of the Canadian Government. Its mission is to ensure that the use of nuclear energy in Canada does not pose undue risk to health, safety, security and the environment.

With much at stake, DCL's stumble out of the starting gate was a disappointment that left Canadian taxpayers on the hook for $100-million and holding an empty heavy water bucket[13].

---

[13] Wilson (Carey) Rudderham lived on the Shore Road in Point Edward, a small farming village bordering the Western branch of Sydney Harbour's Northwest Arm. For many years he served as County Councillor for District 2, Cape Breton County and was well known as a local wit. He showed up at a Council meeting carrying a milk pail with a length of thick rope tied to its handle. When questioned by the County Warden, Carey said in an exaggerated country-farmer twang, *"Follerin' this here meetin' I'm goin' to git me some a that heavy water and I'm gonna' water my tomatoes with it and sell 'em by the pound!"*

# WHAT HAPPENED?

*Based on a Tim Andreeff[14] Story*

The DCL plant problems might have been less harmful if the company had more employees with heavy water plant experience.

The Technical Section had three engineers: two new graduates and the manager. The laboratory had three technicians but no chemist. A chemist was hired but soon left and wasn't replaced. The Production Section had four or five engineers one of whom was a corrosion engineer from Alberta. He was a very pleasant guy, older, and probably good at his job but the younger engineers remembered him by his invitations to dinner and meeting his daughter.

Brown and Root, the construction company, led plant commissioning. They put together a team of experienced oil field operators and chose an experienced engineer to lead it.

An inexperienced Plant Manager led the DCL operating team. One wag opined that the Plant Manager's main qualification was that he had the same initials as the company, DCL. The DCL Production Manager, an older man, suffered from lung cancer and, unfortunately, died on the job. There was a consultant, an American, with a smattering of Savannah River Plant experience.

As plant commissioning began, operating problems mounted, and operators began to question the qualifications of the top team.

All told there were not more than ten qualified DCL engineers during commissioning and start up. There were no specialized engineering teams, for example, process, mechanical, electrical, control, or any of the other important disciplines for start up of a complex chemical plant.

Although not evident, there may have been a start-up plan but there were no written commissioning procedures. Assignments were handed out

---

[14] Author's Note: Tim Andreeff and his wife Lynda Curnoe, sister of acclaimed Canadian artist Greg Curnoe, contributed significantly to this story. A few years ago, my wife Judy and I enjoyed a dinner engagement in Ottawa with Tim and Lynda. Naturally we exchanged stories and memories. To my surprise and delight, I discovered that Tim had worked at the original DCL plant. Our friendship began in the early 1970s when Tim and I worked at the Bruce Heavy Water Plant.

willy-nilly, unrelated to level of experience. In the absence of specific assignments, instructions, or supervision, start-up engineers simply pursued what interested them.

The plant had its share of interesting characters, including a Newfoundland labourer nicknamed Wishy who looked like he just stepped out of a dory. He ran a weekly raffle for a bottle of bootleg rum.

The plant failed spectacularly and was shut down to sort out its many problems. Mother nature got the blame and the preferred explanation of plant failure was salt-water corrosion.

Without doubt, salt water contributed to plant failure. However, there were many other problems and, even if corrosion problems hadn't occurred, the plant still would not have worked. The DCL plant was riddled with design, materials and operating problems. There was blame aplenty.

In hindsight, DCL and their contractors seemed ill prepared to face the complex technical and operating challenges of manufacturing heavy water in Cape Breton.


## SIEVE TRAYS

*Based on a Tim Andreeff Story*

Sieve trays are supposed to capture heavy water[15] but the DCL trays didn't work.

Burns and Roe designed the DCL trays. They had an office in Hempstead Long Island and had a good reputation as designers of power plants. However, they had never designed a heavy water plant. They knew a great deal about steam, water and piping, water treatment, and pressure vessels, but not much about mass transfer and counter-current flows, separation processes and distillation. They hired consultants for what they didn't know.

---

[15] Heavy water plant sieve trays are simply thin metal plates with holes in them. H2S gas passes through the water on the tray resulting in a mixture of gas and water and concentrates deuterium. The arrangement, number and size of the holes in the tray are determined by the required conditions of the chemical process.

Subsequently, DCL engineers expressed a big concern with the performance of the sieve trays and in the summer of 1968, DCL decided to send Tim and Paul to Hempstead for a meeting with Burns and Roe.

This was the first time either had been in New York City, the 'Big Apple'. They shared a cab from the airport and their cab companion, a furtive looking middle-aged man, invited them to a party that evening in downtown Manhattan. Wisely, they turned him down and thus avoided whatever new and strange life experience he had on offer.

Escaping the cab and back on the street, they saw a crowd milling around one of the stores. They were told, in a pronounced local accent, that a group of kids had swarmed a department store, leaving with armfuls of merchandise. Ahh! New York, New York.

The next day, newly alive to the big city, they took the Long Island Railway to Hempstead. They hailed a cab at the train station in Hempstead and watched with surprise as the car ahead of them lost a wheel. The cabbie swerved in and out to avoid the wobbling projectile and subsequently looked in the rear-view mirror at the cowering Canadians. The cabbie laughed and shrugged it off!

When they arrived at the Burns and Roe offices, they were greeted by a Burns and Roe senior design engineer. Once seated in a meeting room and armed with current plant performance data they posed a raft of questions about tray design. Their questions were well intended but the senior designer seemed incensed and accused them of denigrating the entire Burns and Roe process design team.

They assured him of their good intentions and he calmed down. He then arranged for them to meet with their sieve tray consultant, a professor of Chemical Engineering at one of the NY state Universities.

The consultant apparently designed and tested the sieve trays in his basement. His test rig[16] blew air through a 3-foot diameter Plexiglas

---

[16]  *Based on a Tim Andreeff email, May 2018.* The test rig was certainly small compared with the Glitsch rig, the actual size is lost to historical memory. Conducting an atmospheric test is ok - there are well tested fluid mechanical calculations for scaleup. The two test rigs could have agreed but for unknown reasons the results were wildly divergent. This happens in science all the time. It's called unreproducible results. The experience in the plant validated the utility of the Glitsch rig.

column and through holes in the lone sieve tray. The air mixed with water that flowed across the tray. The consultant wanted to prove that his bubbling sieve tray successfully mixed water and air. If so, 'proof' was purely visual. These air-water tests were done at atmospheric pressure and he stretched the results to a plant that was orders of magnitude different in size and process. His simulation did not match 'real world' plant conditions at Glace Bay. It all seemed gloriously stupid to the young engineers.

The DCL trays were manufactured to the consultant's design by Glitsch, a tower and sieve tray manufacturer in Dallas Texas. Glitsch were well equipped with a three-person tech support section, sophisticated calculation procedures and a sophisticated lab for air-water tests. When presented with the tray design by Burns and Roe , Glitsch  challenged the design. Burns and Roe  dismissed their objections and argued that an expert produced their design. Glitsch  then built the DCL trays as instructed.

DCL sent Tim to visit Glitsch to see what could be done to resurrect the failed plant. The first thing Glitsch did was to put three as-built DCL trays into their large test rig. Glitsch 's air water test soon showed why the trays didn't work. Water didn't flow across the trays as it was supposed to. Water passed through the first few bordering holes and splashed onto the tray below. Ninety percent of the gas blew through dry holes. Without sufficient contact between liquid and gas, these trays couldn't capture heavy water.

To calculate tray efficiency, Glitsch injected ammonium into the feed water and analyzed the exit gas for ammonium. Glitsch tried many different tray modifications and they finally got the trays to hold water only by blanking off 90% of the holes. This was a far cry from the original design and a very serious limitation on throughput.

# PASSING GAS

*Based on A Tim Andreeff Story*

$H_2S$ gas is expensive, it costs about $5 per litre at today's prices. Recovering gas from plant outflow water, i.e., effluent, is a good thing to do for economic reasons.

The DCL plant was designed to recover $H_2S$ from the effluent and it used compressors to push the gas back into the plant at 300 pounds pressure. This was done in four successive stages using four flash drums and four compressors.

Each compressor fed gas into the next compressor and the last compressor pushed the gas back into the plant. All four compressors ran off a single drive shaft. DCL operating engineers thought it was a peculiar design and did a lot of sweating and head scratching over how to make it work. They concluded that it would only work under very special conditions, but they didn't how to do it, a so called 'known unknown'.

During one abortive attempt the compressors crashed and were badly damaged. After that, there wasn't much appetite for further attempts to recover $H_2S$ in the wastewater using the four-stage system.

# THE EMPIRE CLUB

On January 23, 1969, the Premier of Nova Scotia, Mr. G.I Smith, in an address to the Empire Club in Toronto, studiously avoided any mention of the emerging DCL fiasco while, at the same time, praising CGE's heavy water plant at Port Hawkesbury.

By the summer of 1969, DCL, and the Government of Nova Scotia felt the political weight of the failed plant, dragging them down like Marley's chains.

Prodded by Spevack, the thinly staffed DCL technical team spent months looking at recovery options via alternative modes of operation. They tested many 'what ifs', including how to use salvageable parts of the crippled plant to make some, any, heavy water. Some of the ideas were fanciful. In the end, resuscitation attempts failed, and the plant was pronounced dead, it was an ex-parrot.

Plant failure led to protracted legal battles among DCL, Burns &Rowe and Brown and Root over who was to blame and, more importantly, who would pay. The dispute wound its way through the Canadian court system all the way to the Supreme Court. In the end, surprise, surprise, Canadian taxpayers paid!

# ALBATROSS

*Ambitions are like albatrosses hung around our necks.*

If this were a movie instead of a book, the page would dissolve into swirly lines and a new scene would open...it's November 27, 1970, and, unfortunately, Cape Breton weather hasn't improved. The temperature hovers around 5°C with rain and drizzle and, you guessed it...fog.

The Cape Breton Post had the following words in an editorial that day and used another bird comparison.

*"If Premier Reagan prompts the removal of the Deuterium 'albatross' from around the neck of Nova Scotia he will earn widespread praise."*

Because, DCL failed to produce any heavy water, AECL was forced to buy heavy water from Sweden and Russia. The article discussed prospects for a rescue of the plant to be financed by the federal government through AECL.

Experienced engineers from the highly successful Savannah River Heavy Water Plant, [SRP], were contracted to complete an assessment of the failed DCL plant.

It's perhaps ironic that the very people Jerome Spevack alienated because of his patent dispute now were engaged to perform the autopsy on his now dead plant. SRP's assessment concluded that extensive corrosion by seawater, equipment failures and technical errors meant that substantial modifications would be necessary in any rehabilitation effort.

# COVERT ACTION

*Money solves most problems*
*– Anonymous*

*NOTE: This account is largely fictitious, it describes what might have happened.*

Saturday, February 14, 1970, Valentine's Day, was a clear, cold morning in Halifax, N.S. The day before, Friday, Premier Smith called Frank Covert[17], his 'go-to' lawyer, to arrange a meeting in the Premier's office at 1700 Granville Street. Smith told Covert that he wanted to discuss Spevack's heavy water contract.

Covert followed the heavy water plant story with considerable interest. There was labour turbulence during plant construction and labour relations was a Covert specialty.

In previous conversations with the Premier, Covert knew something of the political difficulties Smith had with the plant in general and with Spevack in particular.

Thus, he was not entirely surprised when he got the call to meet with the Premier.

Covert was a proud Nova Scotian and he understood the political need to rescue the heavy water plant in Glace Bay. The plant gave the province a black eye and the emerging fiasco threatened to bruise Nova Scotia's reputation further.

Spevack's plant failure was, perhaps, the greatest boondoggle suffered by a NS government in recent history. The roller coaster of public opinion on the government's investment was clearly on the downslope and it threatened to plunge further into an electoral abyss with each passing day.

Smith's government was in deep trouble and faced almost certain electoral defeat in a forthcoming election. It was time to call in the cavalry!

A month earlier Covert had celebrated his 62nd birthday. His 40 years with the Halifax law firm of Stewart McKeen found him in the top echelon of legal minds in Canada. He considered Premier Smith a good friend and he felt some kinship with the WWII war hero. Covert and

---

[17] Frank Manning Covert: Fifty Years in the Practice of Law edited by Barry Cahill, by McGill-Queen's University Press, 2004. Page 161.

Smith shared distinguished war records and, over drinks at the Halifax Club on Hollis Street, they sometimes exchanged war stories.

In January 1945, Covert was navigator of an aircraft assigned to attack Grevenbroich, an important railway yard in Germany. He won a DFC and the citation accompanying his Distinguished Flying Cross read as follows,

*As he was setting course, a leakage caused one engine of the aircraft to become unserviceable and the propeller had to be feathered resulting in considerable loss of height. The aircraft was only able to attain minimum bombing height. Despite this, Flying Officer Covert navigated so skilfully that his aircraft arrived at target at the correct time and a successful attack was pressed home.*

Covert parked his late model Buick on Hollis Street and walked to Government House. It was an unusually cold and windy day and Covert raised his collar and adjusted his scarf to mitigate the bone chilling effects of Halifax weather in February.

He tugged at a brass door handle and, with a second pull, he entered Government House, the official home of the Premier.

He was welcomed in the lobby by Stewart Herald, the Commissionaire. Herald was a WW2 Veteran who was wounded on D-day. Covert came to know and respect the quiet, taciturn man.

"Hi Frank," said Herald, in a familiar tone. "Meeting the boss?"

"Yes, Is he in?" Covert replied.

"Been in since 6 this morning, works like a dog!" Herald replied.

"How have you been?" Covert asked.

"Can't complain," was the reply. Herald shifted uncomfortably in his chair. His wrist had been arthritically complaining since yesterday. Following the D-Day landing, a sniper round passed through his wrist and damaged the joint.

"I'd better get up there then," Covert said, and walked to the elevator.

Weekend work was normal for Covert and for Premier Smith as well. There was something to be said for the quiet hush of the office and the absence of people. Covert accomplished three times as much work on weekends as through the week. Mary, his wife of 36 years was used to the long hours, the weekend work, the sudden changes in plans and the disruptions to family life. A family weekend was a precious commodity in the Covert household.

Covert entered the Premier's suite and passed through the empty office of the Premier's secretary. He heard Smith talking on the telephone and paused in the doorway. The premier raised his head, and Covert caught Smith's attention. Smith nodded, covered the mouthpiece, and gestured to an upholstered chair in front of his large mahogany desk. As he took his seat, Covert's thought, 'you could land the plane on that desk'.

Covert waited for Smith to finish his conversation. Politicians were mostly talkers and few, except for the legally trained, were listeners. While waiting, Covert studied the memorabilia and other bric-a-brac in Smith's office. Great men have great egos and Smith was no exception. The walls sported photos of Smith with Bob Stanfield, John Diefenbaker and General McNaughton.

Covert recalled his longest waiting spell. It was in the office of then Liberal Premier, Henry Hicks, and former President of Dalhousie University. Hicks had a telephone receiver stuffed into his ear and he droned on for 40 minutes in a seemingly endless telephone conversation with an unfortunate bureaucrat. Covert twiddled his thumbs impatiently and amused himself by doing the math on his hourly rate.

Hicks resembled Tweedledum, the chubby character in Lewis Carroll's Alice in Wonderland. He had a big brain but, it seemed, there wasn't enough room for both intellectual musings and politics. Surplus thought bubbled forth in endless chatter. Hicks' Liberal government held power for about two years. An early defeat ended more than twenty years of Liberal hegemony.

Stanfield and his Conservatives won power and now, 14 years later, Smith had succeeded Stanfield and the heavy water fiasco threatened him as well.

Smith finished his telephone conversation moved from behind his desk and sat beside Covert. As far as Covert knew, aside from the security guard, they were the only people in the building that morning.

Smith avoided icebreaking banter and, as was his style, got right to the point. Something had to be done about Spevack.

Smith explained that it was proving difficult to persuade AECL, or anyone else in the Federal Government, to get involved with fixing the plant because of Spevack's reputation as a litigious SOB.

Smith pressed the point that Spevack's intransigence was an obstacle to plant rehabilitation. Several government officials had been thrown into the battle with Spevack and they became little more than legal cannon fodder.

Embarrassingly, Spevack had the province bent over a barrel and he wanted a substantial payout in return for giving the Smith Government a free hand in fixing the DCL mess.

Smith asked Covert to meet with Spevack to get a signed release of claims. Following a few clarifying questions, Covert agreed to meet with Spevack.

Smith pointed to a box of files on a nearby credenza.

"It's all in those files, we need your help, I'm counting on you," said Smith.

"I'll do my best," said Covert.

After parting pleasantries Covert left and took the box of files to his downtown Halifax office to plan his approach.

The following Monday, Covert phoned Spevack to discuss a release of claims to enable plant rehabilitation. To Covert's surprise, Spevack adamantly refused to meet with him or even to discuss a release of claims until he received the money promised to him by the contract. It was a classic 'chicken-and-egg' problem.

Covert's attempts at persuasion seemed to enrage Spevack. Further conversation seemed futile to Covert and, to get some leverage, Covert threatened government legislation to render Spevack's contract null and void.

This tactic got Spevack's attention and he was, at least momentarily, silenced. However, he soon recovered and dismissed the threat.

Covert confidently countered with the suggestion that Spevack engage legal counsel to find out if the Nova Scotia Government had the legal power to do as he had threatened, and he gave Spevack four days to consider it.

The conversation degenerated further and concluded only when Covert threatened to hang up. The tactic worked and Spevack agreed to a meeting with Covert in New York.

Following his telephone call with Spevack, Covert worked on the wording of a release of claims.

Given the nature of Spevack's claims, Covert engaged an experienced patent lawyer to accompany him to the forthcoming meeting in New York.

During the meeting in New York, Spevack began by criticizing Covert's proposed release of claims and he said that he would not sign it unless he got his money beforehand.

The conversation went back and forth with Spevack growing increasingly belligerent. Finally, Covert threatened to leave and advise the government to pass legislation to render the contract null and void. More haggling ensued but eventually the release of claims was verbally agreed although Spevack refused sign it then and there.

Covert returned to Nova Scotia without a signed release. However, he felt that, sooner or later, Spevack would sign once money was on the table.

Later, Spevack and his wife, Ruth[18] met Covert in Halifax. Spevack continued his tirades but relented when Covert again issued an ultimatum.

Fortunately, Ruth urged Jerome to sign. Ruth Spevack proved to be a redoubtable 'Clemmie' to Spevack's stubborn Churchill. Apparently, she had had enough of the tirades, the haggling, the stress and strain associated with the Nova Scotia heavy water plant issue. Ruth Spevack was a shrewd and powerful lawyer and it was she who persuaded her husband to patent his heavy water production method to their everlasting financial benefit. Hence the adage, 'behind every successful man is a surprised woman!'

Spevack relished the negotiating game with its threats, posturing, haggling, and complaining. His tirades were an integral part his negotiation approach. Although he would receive several million dollars by agreeing to sign a release of claims, he somehow managed to construe winning as losing.

Covert placed two copies of the agreement on the table and invited Spevack to sign. Spevack huffed and puffed, and with heavy sighs and much muttering, he patted the pockets of his suit jacket and looked at Ruth with a helpless gesture. Ruth betrayed none of the exasperation she may have felt at that moment. She reached into her purse and handed he husband a fountain pen.

Covert, a keen observer in moments like this recognized the pen as a Graf von Faber-Castel Pen, among the best in the world.

---

[18] Ruth Spevack was Secretary-Treasurer and a Director. of Deuterium Corporation, the US's parent company, of which her husband Jerome was President. and Chairman.

With a flourish, Spevack removed the cap and glowered at Covert. With pen poised above the bottom line of the document, he said he was 'damned glad' to be rid of 'that cursed plant'.

To Covert's relief, Spevack signed the release of claims. Covert retrieved the signed document, signed a cheque, and offered it to Jerome. Ruth Spevack took the cheque and put it in her purse, as though afraid that her husband might misplace it. This was the first of many payments to Spevack. By agreement, payments would be spread over several years.

Spevack was out and the Government controlled DCL Board of Directors subsequently engaged AECL to manage the plant's rehabilitation.

But first, Nova Scotia Premier, G.I. Smith had to face the Legislature and get approval for a motion to proceed at once with the rehabilitation of the Heavy Water Plant at Glace Bay.

# FLUMMERY

*"It's an unconstitutional piece of flummery[19] to come in here and ask
this Legislature to put the seal of approval on a decision that this
Government has irrevocably made. I wish we would have been spared this
terrible, terrible millstone, this financial millstone, around our necks for
generations to come."*
*- Peter Nicholson: MLA, Annapolis West*


Lt. Col. the Hon. G. I. Smith, M.B.E., E.D., Q.C., Premier of Nova
Scotia, took his place in the legislative chamber of Province House, the
locus of government. Forty of the forty-six seats were already occupied.
He was among the last to appear, as was his privilege. The date was April
21, 1970, and the temperature outside inched towards 5C. The temperature
inside was warm and, before the day was out, it would be hot.

Premier Smith looked across the floor at Gerald Regan, leader of the
Liberal Party, the Loyal Opposition. Regan leaned forward and made eye
contact with the Premier, challenging him. Then, he smiled, licked his lips
and whispered something to Peter Nicholson, the Liberal member from
Annapolis West, his best oratorical weapon.

Premier Smith dreaded the protracted debate and the long day ahead.
He opened the sealed folder on his desk and scanned the motion he would
put before the House.

*The Motion is Resolved that the House hereby approve the decision of
the Government to accept a recommendation of the Board of Directors of
Deuterium of Canada Limited, that the Corporation be authorized to
proceed at once with the rehabilitation of this Heavy Water Plant at Glace
Bay. Moved by the Honourable the Premier, seconded by the Honourable
the Attorney General.*

The motion proposed that a $30 million rehabilitated rabbit could be
yanked from the government's magic, yet frayed, fedora.

---

[19] flummery

noun (pl. flummeries) empty compliments; nonsense: she hated the
flummery of public relations. ORIGIN early 17th cent. from Welsh
llymru; perhaps related to llymrig 'soft, slippery.

The speaker brought the assembly to order. Smith glanced to his right and nodded to Attorney General, Richard Donahue.

Donahue, an experienced politician and a top-notch lawyer, turned towards Smith and flashed a confident smile. A smile Smith had seen many times before. Donahue was ready...the Tory Party was ready. Ready to bring Jerome Spevack's politically disastrous plant under their wing.

The motion passed but not before Government members, especially the Premier, was liberally chewed on by the opposition.

Smith recalled the words of a long dead politician who, following a particularly gruelling debate, said; it was "...like being nibbled to death by ducks."

Smith succeeded Robert Lorne (Bob) Stanfield, a revered political figure in Nova Scotia and now, in 1970, the Leader of Her Majesty's Loyal Opposition in the Parliament of Canada. Stanfield had a shot at being Prime Minister of Canada but was outfoxed by Pierre Trudeau, the father of Canada's current Prime Minister, Justin Trudeau.

In a minor but unfortunate leadership campaign moment, Stanfield was photographed eating a banana ... a most unflattering picture. The photo didn't swing the election, but it didn't help. In another photographed gaffe, Stanfield executed a ceremonial kick-off at a football game and fumbled the ball, another unfortunate metaphorical moment.

Stanfield's departure from Nova Scotia politics preceded a 'coming-home-to-roost' of political problems; the threatened closure of the steel plant in Sydney and the failure of Peter Munk's Clairtone, a manufacturer of televisions and sound systems in Stellarton.

Now, to top it off, there was this damned heavy water plant in Glace Bay.

As was his nature, Smith addressed these problems decisively and, not for the first time, he felt the full weight of his office.

At times like this Smith might have been grateful for his World War II experience where, more than once, he was mentioned in dispatches for meritorious action in the face of the enemy. Political battles were, however, fought with words, not guns, and there were damned few medals.

The Liberal opposition was small, 6 seats, compared with the government's 40 seats, in a 46-seat legislature. However, and of late, Regan and the other members of the Liberal Party were acting with increased confidence. They wanted to make political hay with heavy water.

Jerome Spevack's heavy water plant was, at the very least, a problem, a political, and economic, disaster.

Spevack's intransigence about his exit compensation was a big problem for the Smith government. A question arose in Smith's mind, 'are some folks rich because they're assholes are they assholes because they're rich?'

As problems with the plant grew in size, Spevack proved a very difficult person to deal with. By all accounts, he was narcissistic, argumentative, and litigious. He sued the United States government over patent infringement and legal experts predicted he might win. If so, this meant a Spevack windfall of millions.

Deuterium of Canada Limited promised heavy water in 1966. Now, In April 1970, four years later, not a drop was evident.

Smith's government was attempting a rescue and rehabilitation of Spevack's failed plant, with considerable financial help from Alan McEachern and the federal government. Together they agreed to commit tens of millions of dollars of taxpayer's money.

Smith's government was in a deliciously tight political spot and Gerald Reagan knew it.

There were few options open to the government. A study by E. I. du Pont de Nemours and Company, SRP, estimated it would take at least $30 million and two years of work to bring the plant into production. With an election in the offing, abandoning the project and dining on politically-baked crow was out of the question.

In early May 1967, the DCL plant was 'officially' opened with all the bagpiping and hullabaloo a Nova Scotia Government could muster. Dignitaries of all shapes and sizes, from near and far, puffed up and converged on the hardscrabble coal-mining town of Glace Bay. Federal and Provincial politicians clawed their way to the forefront. The only 'star' missing was...yep...you guessed it... heavy water... because not a drop of the much-anticipated heavy water had been produced, nada, zip, zero.

An election was held later that month and Smith's party won handily. Mission accomplished, now what!

Spevack was a troublesome variable in the plant rehabilitation equation. AECL and the Nova Scotia Government feared he might yank yet another patent infringement lawsuit from his stockpile of heavy water litigation opportunities. His lawsuit against the United States Government was dragging through American courts and his litigious approach to business cast a shadow over the plant rehabilitation project.

The DCL plant failed to produce any heavy water and yet Spevack claimed full payment of his $3 million fee. The government needed a signed release of all claims from Spevack to proceed with plant rehabilitation.

Early in 1970, in a very private meeting, Smith asked Nova Scotia's most reputable litigator, Frank Covert, to find a legal way to send Spevack packing. Marshalling his considerable skills as a legal persuader, Covert got Spevack to sign a release, presumably in return for payment of his fee, a rumoured $3 million.

The opposition was bound to pounce on this issue. And pounce they did!

*Gerald Reagan led off...*

*"In all my time in this Legislature, Mr. Speaker, I have never seen such a startling proposition as what this Government expects this Legislature to do in respect of this Resolution. First, they announce in the Resolution that the Government has decided, an executive decision, to go and rebuild that plant.*

*They say that the decision was based on a recommendation of the Board of Directors of Deuterium of Canada. Mr. Speaker, Deuterium of Canada is nothing more nor less than this Government and, no matter how they squirm and twist, they can't get out from under that fact. This Government owns the plant lock, stock and barrel. ...It fired the President. It paid him off with $3 million and sent him back to the United States ...Remember the Honourable Premier expressing hope of having heavy water for Christmas, a year ago last Christmas, do you remember, prior to that, the official opening of a plant in the Spring of 1967, which three years later hasn't produced a drop of heavy water."*

*Peter Nicholson joined the attack...*

*"It's an unconstitutional piece of flummery to come in here and ask this Legislature to put the seal of approval on a decision that this Government has irrevocably made.*

*I wish we would have been spared this terrible, terrible millstone, this financial millstone, around our necks for generations to come. Mr.*

*Spevack himself was recognized as having the best process in the world. How then, with this nice package of goods, how then with this fine and almost pristine piece of technology, did they manage in the years to mess it up so badly?*

*The Premier of the day, then the Honourable R.L. Stanfield, said that the best process in the world for producing heavy water, and the only proven process, was that of Jerome Spevack, and we accepted that at the time, and I think that he was quite honest in making that assessment. Perhaps it is the best process. I'm prepared to believe that, and having believed it, I can't imagine how much bungling it took to waste $112 million to this date in a plant that has not produced one ounce of heavy water since the three years that it's been opened.*

*[H]ow the thing was bungled after all these arrangements he made in 1963 about having Mr. McEachern carry the ball ... Perhaps McEachern carried it part of the way, but when he threw it ... right out of the ball park and it hasn't been recovered since.*

*How much misinformation - how much negligence - how much recklessness had to go along with a situation, ... to turn what was the hope of commerce, into the despair of defeat, and into the kind of a grovelling Resolution that this Government has presented to this House.*

*I remember, Mr. Speaker, very well, the afternoon that the Premier got up in this House and ...he introduced a Bill to provide for further funds for Deuterium of Canada Limited, and that was the beginning of the long and sorry tale of the Government ownership of this ill-fated plant. ...it was $18 million down the drain.*

*At the time that this shift was made, there was still some hope and expectation that heavy water would be a reality in Nova Scotia... that won't cost them $124 million which is the best, it seems to me, that we can hope for now.*

*I just hope that that industry succeeds. ...But the sad and sorry history, Sir, has been that every time anything succeeds in this province, the Government takes the credit for it ...Every time it fails, they come running to the Legislature ...to try to patch it up.*

*They've made a deal with the Government of Canada, they've made a deal with the AECL, they've made a deal with the Board of Directors of Deuterium, who are their puppets, and they've made deals with everybody all along the line, ... and then they come in and ask us to put the seals on it for them.*

*(I recall a Chambers)... cartoon...there were two chimneys, and Santa was coming up to the chimneys with a heavy water plant on his back, and it was entitled 'Santa's Dilemma', because he didn't know whether to go down the western chimney, or the eastern chimney, I just hope he had gone down the western chimney, I wish he had, Mr. Speaker, with all the heart I have, I wish he had and that we would have been spared this terrible, terrible millstone, this financial millstone, around our necks for generations to come. "*

The resolution was put before the House for a vote. The government's overwhelming majority carried the day and the resolution passed.

MR. SPEAKER:

Before the Honourable Gentleman proceeds, could the Member for Annapolis West tell me what "flummery" means?

MR. NICHOLSON:

Yes, that's a contraction of the phrase, "flimming and flamming", which sometimes is called but I prefer to call it flummery. It's a ...

MR. SPEAKER:

It's a word of the Honourable Gentleman's own invention,

MR. NICHOLSON:

Oh, indeed it is not, it's a good old English word, flummery is, and I think the Premier will support me on that.

MR. SPEAKER:

My problem is whether it's Parliamentary. That's ...

MR. NICHOLSON:

Oh, I'm ·sure it is, it's quite a polite word.

THE PREMIER:

Mr. Speaker, I'm sure it's Parliamentary, because it exactly describes what we've just listened to. (Laughter)

# RISE AGAIN

Like the Phoenix, the bird-creature of Greek mythology, the DCL plant died in a show of combustible gas, corrosion and constipation[20]. The Canadian government's decision to award a heavy water production contract to DCL over AECL's objections proved disastrous for all concerned. By all accounts, the Government of Nova Scotia was especially embarrassed[21].

The Province of Nova Scotia assumed ownership and control of the plant and sought help in rehabilitating it.

Experienced engineers from the highly successful Savannah River Heavy Water Plant, [SRP], completed an assessment of the failed DCL plant. It's ironic that the very people Jerome Spevack avoided because of his patent dispute turned out to be the people who did the autopsy on his failed plant. The SRP experts concluded that extensive corrosion by seawater, equipment design and operating errors required substantial modifications to what remained of DCL if the plant was to perform as a viable heavy water production facility.

A tortuous political process ensued and eventually AECL inherited the still smouldering remains. With an acute shortage of heavy water needed for Canada's nuclear power development, the federal government provided an additional $41.5-million so that AECL could sift through DCL's ashes and fix the failed plant.

In 1971, AECL assumed full control of the plant. It was a major undertaking to re-create a viable heavy water plant from the ruins of the DCL plant. It had to be a new thing. As the Biblical parable says, new wine must be put into new skins...if only it were that easy. AECL's rehabilitation project benefited from the full support of Canadian and US expertise in heavy water plant design, production, and operation. Through

---

[20] In Greek Mythology a phoenix is a long-lived bird that is cyclically regenerated or reborn. A phoenix obtains new life by arising from the ashes of its predecessor.

[21] Years later, a member of the housekeeping staff in the Nova Scotia Legislature talked about supplies for cabinet meetings at that time. He said, "They gobbled handfuls of Aspirin and drank gallons of Alka-Seltzer."

an agreement with the USAEC, there was an exchange of personnel and know-how in heavy water production. The Canadian plants exchanged personnel for training and consulting purposes. A consulting engineering company, Canatom MonMax, was engaged to re-design and rebuild the plant, starting in 1972.

# REHAB

The gambler's secret to survival about knowing what to keep and what to throw away applies to the rehabilitation of busted heavy water plants. Survival in this case meant saving money by reusing original DCL plant equipment.

Critical changes were planned for the DCL plant. These changes meant a new process and a switch from salt water to fresh water as the source of heavy water and for cooling of equipment. Given a new design opportunity, Canatom MonMax process engineers also decided to 'tweak' some features and 'tweaking' proved risky, as AECL soon found out[22].

The need for good technical support[23] was first recognized when CGE's Port Hawkesbury Heavy Water plant ran into difficulty in the early stages of its operation.

Until then it was assumed that the scaled-up Canadian plants would perform at least as well as the US Atomic Energy Commission Plant at Savannah River, South Carolina. However, the 'scaling factor' proved a challenge. The Port Hawkesbury plant at 400 tons per year capacity was 16 times larger than the SRP heavy water production units.

---

[22] In the years that followed, Canadian plants benefited from a supportive R&D effort spearheaded by the AECL Team at Chalk River, led by Howard Rae. Thanks to important contributions from Al Bancroft, Martin Galley and Alastair Miller, Canadian plants received strong scientific and technical support.

[23] Frank Kober was one of the support staff. He was employed by Canatom-Monmax during construction and worked in the inspection department. He left when the rehab work was completed and the first H2S railcar arrived to 'charge' the plant prior to start-up. He accepted a job in Sydney as a field supervisor in a home construction company. It was a good position for several years until interest rates went to 24% + and the company folded. He was fortunate to get work at AECL in the maintenance department doing planning, estimating and scheduling for all trades. He was particularly good at planning shutdown jobs. Shutdown planning involved estimating trades effort and comparing it to actual. Frank spent eight years with AECL.

# GLACE BAY TRAINEES

The rehab project for the plant at Glace Bay was well underway when a dozen young Cape Bretoners arrived at the Toronto International Airport. They were a mix of rookie and experienced plant operators, newly hired by AECL for the Glace Bay plant. They were headed for the Bruce Heavy Water Plant, [BHWP], to learn plant operations before returning to the Glace Bay plant. Most of them were native Nova Scotians eager to prove their operating knowledge and skills.

They collected their luggage and waited outside for a bus that would take them to a motel in the town of Kincardine, 200 km away, on the shores of Lake Huron.

At 7:00 AM the following Monday their bus turned left off Highway 21 and entered the access road leading to the BHWP. In the distance, they saw the shimmering waters of Lake Huron and, reaching skyward, the tall towers of the BHWP.

The bus passed a large parking lot, packed with the hundreds of cars of belonging to the 6000 construction workers on the Bruce site. They were building the adjacent nuclear power plant and a large heavy water plant expansion. Acres of white-clad 40-foot trailers housed and fed live-in construction workers. It was an impressive sight.

They were about to be, albeit temporarily, part of one of the world's most extensive nuclear power development programs and their prospects were exciting.

The bus pulled into a parking lot in front of a concrete-grey two-story Administration and Control building. Paul Core and Jim Dalton, two of BHWP's most experienced shift supervisors, met them at the door.

They spent their first day in an orientation session in the Training Centre. They studied a detailed scale model of the Bruce Plant, built at a cost of half million dollars. They had a brief tour of the Control Room and received their shift assignments. They reported the next day for shift work and spent the rest of the summer learning operator duties.

It was Ontario Hydro's practice in those days, to roster five shifts instead of the usual four. This allowed for a 'supernumerary' shift and enabled operators to spend at least 20% of their time going to school in the Training Centre, learning how to operate the plant. Courses on, pumps, blowers, heat exchangers, piping, electrical control system instrumentation, chemistry were required of every operator. Progress was measured, and promotion through the ranks of operator was, in part, dependent upon the employee's training record.

These young men were smart and eager and acquitted themselves well while at BHWP. So much so that some Shift Supervisors asked Production Manager Bill Hatton whether they couldn't "steal" them. That wasn't on.

A few months later, with their training complete, the operators returned to GBHWP ready to put their newly acquired skills into practice.

# SETBACK

*Spevack cursed this 'friggin' plant!*

*-Anonymous*

The newly rehabilitated Glace Bay began a limited operation in May 1975 when the distillation system was used to upgrade diluted heavy water from the BHWP. In January 1976, the plant was again filled with hundreds of tons of hydrogen sulphide gas. Six months later, on 15 June 1976, the plant produced reactor grade heavy water. This important milestone occurred 10 years later than Spevack had promised following a multi-million-dollar makeover.

The first hint of what some felt was 'Spevack's Curse'[24] occurred in mid-July 1976 when a small H2S gas leak in a heat exchanger forced a partial system shutdown. By mid-September, the plant was back in operation and within two months the plant was operating near design conditions. By Christmas of 1976, the optimism of plant employees was palpable.

On December 29, 1976, tragedy struck, and spirits crushed when three workers were overcome by H2S when attempting to clear a blockage at the base of the 400-foot flare stack[25].

The official accident report praised the effective response of rescuers but said that the workers should have worn better protective breathing equipment.

---

[24] Spevack's Curse. The Glace Bay plant had more problems than any other Canadian heavy water plant. One possible explanation of Spevack's curse was the plant's use of salt water. The idea that spilling salt is unlucky is a common superstition handed down from ancient times. One widespread explanation is that Judas Iscariot spilled the salt of the Last Supper. Leonardo da Vinci's painting depicts Judas having knocked over a salt-cellar. Salt was a valuable commodity in ancient times and came to symbolize different values and was often used in religious rituals. Even today, superstitious people will throw a pinch of salt over their left shoulder to ward off bad luck associated with spilled salt.

[25] The flare stack is a critical piece of safety infrastructure for heavy water plants. It can quickly and effectively 'flare' or 'burn' the entire contents of the plant in the event of a serious H2S leak.

One of the men, Barry Burke[26], 19, suffered very serious brain damage and although he survived, he never fully recovered.

Things went from bad to worse at the plant when several more heat exchangers[27], leaked H2S.

The tragic accident and the heat exchanger leaks forced the AECB to suspend the plant's operating license. From that point onward, AECB had to be persuaded that the plant was safe to operate. The AECB had the plant under a microscope.

The situation made for difficult decisions by AECL's board, led by Chairman Ross Campbell.

Fortunately for plant employees and a community desperate for jobs, their Member of Canada's Parliament was Alan J. McEachen, Trudeau's Deputy Prime Minister. McEachen was sympathetic to the pleas of constituents that the plant must be saved.

The President of AECL, at that time was Dr. John Foster. He was a Nova Scotian engineer with a distinguished record in the development of nuclear power. Having experienced the ups and downs of nuclear power, Foster took the long view and, being an engineer, he said that Canada's heavy water production problems would be fixed.

---

[26] Barry Burke passed away on December 26, 2013, 37 years later, at the age of 56. The other two workers, Frank Greene and Steve Royal, where treated in a local hospital and fully recovered.

[27] The decision to reuse original DCL designed heat exchangers might be characterized as a 'bad' engineering decision. However, it's conceivable that if replacement of all 24 heat exchangers was recommended the cost might have doomed the project from the start.

# PULL THE PLUG?

*Based on a Gerry Armitage Story*

In 1976, the AECL Board of Directors dispatched board member, Donald J. Smith[28], CEO of Ellis-Don Construction, to obtain a first-hand, 'boots on the ground', assessment of the plant situation. Gerry Armitage guided Don Smith through an inspection of the plant. Smith surveyed the situation, particularly the corroded shells of heat exchangers, and bluntly asked, "Is it time to pull the plug on this plant?"

Don Smith's reaction perhaps reflected the mindset of the AECL board and its then Chairman/President, Ross Campbell. The board endured fourteen years of promises and disappointments. They had to account for the expenditure of many millions of taxpayer's dollars. A 'here-we-go-again' reaction was not unlikely.

Don Smith's existential question was obvious although most plant employees wanted a chance to prove they could make the plant work.

The enthusiastic 1963 announcement in the Cape Breton Post of, "...the biggest industrial complex in Cape Breton since the turn of the century," seemed, fourteen years later, to be not much more than home town boosterism. The much-maligned plant was an embarrassment that had yet to prove it could produce heavy water.

DEVCO, the Cape Breton coal mining enterprise, another ward of the Federal government would also be seriously affected by closure of the heavy water plant. Heavy water production required thousands of tons of Cape Breton coal supplied to Nova Scotia's power utility, NSP. Hundreds of jobs in coal mining and power production hung in the balance: in Alan J. McEachern's constituency.

A decision to commit further taxpayer funds for the twice-failed GBHWP was, presumably, a difficult one for the AECL Board and its

---

[28]  Donald Smith's Toronto based company is best known for construction of the Sky Dome, now known as the Rogers Center, home of the Toronto Blue Jays. The Sky Dome had the world's first retractable roof stadium. It was Don Smith's signature achievement. Smith died on July 16, 2013 at 89 years of age.

banker, the Government of Canada. However, *mirabile dictu*[29], money for repair and restart was found. Alan J McEachern, one-time St.F.X. lecturer in economics, Cape Breton MP and, in 1977, Deputy Prime Minister, weighed in and politics trumped economics!

Arrayed against this dismal AECL backdrop was the growing success of Ontario Hydro's heavy water plants. Beginning in 1973 the BHWP was producing a ton or more of reactor grade heavy water every day. Ontario Hydro planned to build several additional heavy water plants of the BHWP design. The large and growing heavy water production capacity of Ontario Hydro slowly nudged AECL's Cape Breton plants to the sidelines[30].

---

[29] Latin Expression, often used by my grade 12 teacher, Bernadette Francis. whenever I surprised her with a decent mark in French: Wonderful to tell. in the vernacular: surprise, surprise!

[30] The Cape Breton plants ceased production in 1985. Ontario Hydro produced another 3000 tons of heavy water from 1986 until 1990.

# THREE BIG CHALLENGES

In 1976 and into 1977, Hugh VanAlstyne, the newly appointed General Manager, and his leadership team[31],[32]faced three big challenges to overcome in their quest for a viable plant.

•Corroded heat exchangers.

•A restricted operating license.

•Process plant instability.

Any one of these would tax the courage and ingenuity of the operating team. Taken together, they forecast a challenging year ahead.

---

[31] Gerry Armitage, Production Manager, Arthur Pratt, Maintenance Manager, Bob Brown, Head of Administration, Frank tenTusscher, Head of Finance, Gerry Coleman, Purchasing Manager and Rollie MacInnis, Technical Manager.

[32] Rollie MacInnis was recruited in 1977. As Gerry Armitage said, later on, *"When Hugh first came as General manager at Glace Bay, we discussed what needed to be done and replacing the Technical Manager was the top priority."*

# JIM WRIGHT'S FIX

The plant production process environment, i.e., inside the equipment, is acidic... think sulphuric acid. At SRP, flow rates were carefully controlled so as not to erode a protective iron sulphide layer coating the carbon steel innards. By 1976, at Glace Bay, this hot, acidic liquid had eaten its way through the thick carbon steel walls of some heat exchangers[33].

These were the same heat exchangers originally used by DCL but were 'saved' during rehab, probably to cut costs. The original design was a poor choice for the conditions of the Glace Bay plant.

The heat exchanger corrosion problem topped the list of challenges to the viability of the plant. Replacement of all heat exchangers was out of the question since the cost was prohibitive. The plant was doomed if the heat exchangers could not be repaired.

Fortunately, the mechanical engineering group, led by Jim Wright, developed an innovative and affordable solution. This involved welding layers of hardened stainless steel over the 'corrosion zone'.

Twenty-four heat exchangers were removed and shipped to Great Lakes Fabricating in Sarnia, Ontario, 1500 miles away. Although the repair project cost several million dollars, it was much less than the cost of replacing heat exchangers.

The question, 'will this repair work?' was uppermost in the minds of VanAlstyne's team and, not surprisingly, in the minds of the AECB. Fortunately, it did!

Heavy water production continued on a restricted basis under a temporary operating licence while repairs were carried out.

---

[33] These were so called 'shell and tube' heat exchangers. A tube bundle fits within a cylindrical shell. The liquids flowing through shell and tube are at different temperatures. Hence 'heat exchange'.
Corrosion/erosion occurred along the midline of the shell wall, caused by fast flowing liquid.

# ICELY ASSESSMENT

In mid-1977, with the viability of the plant in doubt, VanAlstyne invited Bob Icely, Plant Manager of Ontario Hydro's BHWP[34], to assemble a team of experts to study the operation and recommend improvements.

In hindsight this was courageous because it exposed the sins of past and current plant operators. It turned out to be a lesson in handling a difficult situation, *i.e., ask for help and don't constrain the 'helpers'.*

Icely's, team included Bill Hatton, General Manager of Port Hawkesbury Heavy Water Plant, [PHHWP], , JC Paquin, General Manager of the LaPrade plant, and process and equipment experts from the Bruce Plant, e.g., Bob Gibson, and scientific staff from AECL Chalk River, Dr. Al Bancroft, Dr. Martin Galley, and Dr. Alastair Miller[35].

Icely's team got down to business very quickly. During the weeklong assessment they visited the plant each day, pored over plant operating data, and interviewed key members of VanAlstyne's team.

Each evening, VanAlstyne's team met Icely's team in an AECL Apartment at Cabot House, on King's Road in Sydney to discuss results. Notwithstanding critical comments, conversations flowed freely, and ideas were discussed in a spirit of cooperation. The Icely team submitted their report in a remarkably short time. There were many practical recommendations for improvement and most of them were implemented in the following months.

The thrust of Icely's report was that plant performance would be significantly improved if several task force recommendations were implemented without delay.

One of the important observations was,

"The Glace Bay team has done a commendable job in identifying problems. However, they have been slow to develop and implement

---

[34] In discussing the successful commissioning program at the Bruce heavy water plant, Howard Rae credits "...the outstanding leadership of R.F.U Icely... "

[35] Miller was an 'ask-me-anything' math guy with a Hewlett-Packard calculator strapped to his belt.

solutions." Managers must act, not just study, analyse and ponder. In other words, Do something!

VanAlstyne's subsequent decisions based on the Icely team's recommendations played a vital role in the future success of the plant.

At VanAlstyne's request, Martin Galley was seconded to the plant to help with plan implementation. Galley developed effective working relationships with plant operators and acted as liaison between the engineers at the plant and the scientists at Chalk River. An important Galley recommendation was that process improvement projects be implemented in a recommended sequence and not 'cherry picked'. He helped both scientists and engineers negotiate process performance testing. For example, a Chalk River scientist might ask that a process sample be taken from a 'sample point' located high among the maze of piping and vessels. Galley understood that asking an operator to climb 150 feet up at 2 o'clock in the morning during a February blizzard might not be a good idea if the test sample could be taken at a more favourable time.

# NEW PLAN

Using the recommendations of the Icely report, VanAlstyne's team developed a plan to improve production. Each major problem, e.g., heat exchanger corrosion, was categorized by its effect on heavy water production. The larger the effect, the higher the priority.

In a perfect world, industrial plants would operate as designed, at 100 percent capacity, forever. Even the best run plants encounter unforeseen events, for example, a power failure resulting in reduced capacity.

Improvement projects were carefully planned so that labour and equipment could be brought to bear quickly to take advantage of every opportunity.

The need for current information on important aspects of plant operations was emphasized. Frank tenTussher, prepared a weekly report with key performance indicators. This report included information on production, energy use, spending, and several aspects of human resources, such as safety.

Plant performance trends were closely watched, and adverse trends were quickly corrected. Collecting and using 'good information' enabled a focus on important elements of performance.

In subsequent years, equipment reliability improved, interruptions occurred less often. Production increased in 1977, doubled in 1978 and rose above 200 Megagrams, [tons], per year for the next few years.

By the early 1980s Canadian heavy water production began to exceed demand and a growing surplus became evident.

# AECB LICENCE

Convincing the AECB to lift restrictions on the plant's operating license was a vital step in the plan to enable heavy water production.

In 1976 and well into 1977, AECB inspectors made regular visits to the plant. They asked questions and demanded reports. AECB Inspectors challenged plant explanations at every turn. Sometimes it was difficult to respond to some AECB suggestions[36].

Heat exchanger corrosion dominated the AECB agenda since cracks or holes in these exchangers meant that poisonous hydrogen sulphide gas could escape. The concept of 'leak before failure' means that small leaks can be detected and stopped before catastrophic failure and a large gas release. However, no plant wanted to make that idea the foundation of their safety program. Leak prevention via regular inspection is the key.

The mission of the heavy water plant inspection team was to ensure that equipment would not fail and release H2S. Assurance of the physical integrity of the plant was provided via an approved inspection program. Most inspections are non-invasive, i.e., while the plant is operating. Non-destructive techniques such as ultrasound serve this purpose[37].

Under normal circumstances the AECB responds favourably to sound technical arguments based on well-established industry practice. The chequered history of the plant and the disastrous events of December 1976 meant that almost any inspection plan was met with skepticism.

Unfortunately, the inspection supervisor at that time, was 'an alarmist', an attention getter. He was the 'Henny Penny' of the plant and the 'sky was always falling'. Somehow, he persuaded the AECB that a thermal imaging inspection technique would detect exchanger corrosion. Upon closer examination, this approach relied on very small differences in temperature to show wall thickness changes. Research into the physics of thermal

---

[36] At one such meeting Hugh VanAlstyne emitted a 'creative sneeze'. The AECB representative suggested after which Hugh took couple of deep breaths as though he was going to sneeze and emitted a sneeze-like outburst that sounded very much like 'horseshit'.

[37] Plant inspectors were, Bill Rankin, George Yih, Bill 'Gizmo' MacKenzie and Billy McMullin. Billy McMullin went on to set up his own inspection company.

imaging showed that this approach couldn't work. It was virtually impossible to detect a few thousandths of an inch of corrosion by imaging the outside of a hot heat exchanger. Thermal imaging inspection was a 'thin reed' on which to assure the AECB. Thus, a better method, i.e., ultrasound was developed in 1977[38].

In mid-1977 the AECB wanted to discuss heat exchanger inspection methods and to consider whether, given successful heat exchanger repairs, a less restrictive operating license might be granted.

A meeting with a plant presentation was arranged with the Board itself. This was highly unusual since such presentations are normally made in writing to the AECB staff who then makes recommendations to the Board. By asking for a presentation to the Board, the AECB signalled that this was a very serious situation requiring highly convincing arguments for license renewal. The meeting with AECB went ahead and thermal imaging was nudged into the background although not dropped entirely. Ultrasound was accepted as the primary means of integrity assurance. The AECB approved an operating license but added a condition that required the plant to install a Gas Dispersion System, GDS[39].

Creating more effective relationships with regulators, especially the AECB, became an important goal in 1977. Fred Hill, Plant Chemist, was reassigned to the newly created position of Regulatory Manager. Fred did an excellent job at this. He exuded integrity and was a thoughtful communicator and not given to 'running off at the mouth'. He spoke when spoken to, answered questions, and volunteered only what was necessary. Fred was the perfect person to be working with regulatory agencies. This new arrangement enabled several regulatory agencies to be managed in a more consistent way.

---

[38] Author's Note: This technique was implemented prior to my arrival and was one of the first things I challenged.

[39] GDS: Gas Dispersion System. A ring of high-energy propane burners encircling the plant were designed to fire up and create an updraft to disperse H2S. Bob Sissingh, a BHWP Senior Engineer, visited the plant to investigate the need for the so-called 'ring of fire'. Bob said, "Johnny Cash sang about it! I did not recommend it, [they did it anyway]."

# PROBLEM SOLVING

*"We finally trained the mule to work without eating...then it up and died."*

*– Anonymous*

Throughout 1977, employees solved problems, fixed things, figured things out, learned and persisted. Progress was slow and there were setbacks but soon the plant operated at or near design conditions.

Failed heat exchangers and the risk of a poisonous gas release topped management's agenda. Not surprisingly, the Atomic Energy Control Board had the plant on a short leash because of years of failure and bad press.

Intense anti-nuclear protests were now in the public eye. Failures at Three-Mile Island in the USA and Chernobyl in the then Soviet Union were in the news. AECL countered emotive antinuclear protests with facts about risk. However, for some people, facts are not usually persuasive[40].

Employees were determined to prove something, and the plant made progress every day.

Atomic Energy of Canada Limited, were, nominally, the owners of the plant but, it was the Government of Canada that paid the bills. In those days, there must have been some interesting conversations taking place in the corridors of power in Ottawa.

---

[40] The risk of cutting your life short by being 30 pounds overweight is 2000 times greater than the risk of cutting your life short by living near a nuclear plant. Generally speaking, people worry more about nuclear accidents than of being overweight.

# PRODUCTION

Newly repaired heat exchangers were installed and to everyone's relief, the repair was very successful. For the first time in years, the plant was producing reactor-grade heavy water at peak efficiency[41]

Canada's heavy water production crisis was just about over and AECL's supply forecast showed the first glimmers of surplus. However, the looming problem of oversupply was largely unrecognized at the plant level and it was 'full steam ahead'.

The production team finally had a reliable plant to operate and they were determined to prove its capability[42].

The control room was in a stand-alone building close to the operating units. It had wall-to-wall instrument panels with the usual 1970s style dials, gauges, charts, buttons and switches. Desk top screens displayed updated process information from a customized data logger. The control room was also the locus of the plant emergency management system.

Adjacent to the control room was a small meeting room where Technical Department process engineers met with Production staff to review plant performance and make plans. A whiteboard displayed daily production performance[43].

---

[41] *Heavy Water Plant Surpasses Records:* Cape Breton Post, March 30, 1981.

"Over the past three years the Glace Bay Heavy Water Plant has surpassed its production records and exceeded its own production forecast. This improved performance has been the result of modification trays and selected processed hours the use of the new anti-foam agent and greater reliability of plant equipment in fact the plant is producing approximately the same quantity of water for less cost. Plant maintenance and steam availability have contributed to this improved efficiency."

[42] Gerry Armitage's team included Martin Mannion and Shift Supervisors, Ted Tobin, Doug Lewis, Ron Sutherland, Frank Bailey. In May 2004, Frank Bailey passed away. Soccer Nova Scotia lauded his 25-year contribution, seven of which he served as President.

[43] There is an apocryphal story of Andrew Carnegie, the US steel magnate who wrote daily production figures in chalk on the floor of his steel mill to inspire his men to do better.

Thanks to the training and experience of the production staff, the plant operated for longer and longer stretches of time without interruption[44].

# MAINTENANCE

Maintenance of the plant was in the hands of very experienced managers, supervisors, mechanics, control and electrical technicians and other trades.

Many of these people had been with the plant from DCL days. The plant also had a large contract maintenance group from Catalytic Construction, led by Jack Cox.

As plant reliability improved, it became obvious that there were more people in the maintenance department than required and the contract with Catalytic was terminated. Total plant employment level, including contractors, decreased from 478 in 1980 to 323 in1984.

Arthur Pratt was the Maintenance Manager. He was an experienced UK-born engineer with a clever grasp of the budgeting process. His favourite metaphor for money availability was a drawstring purse. He often said, with elaborate hand gestures to emphasize his point, *"When the purse opens best get your hand in and out quickly lest it pull shut and cut you off."*

The Mechanical Supervisor was Mancel Smith. He was assisted by maintenance foremen, Jack Stevens and Gerry McSween. Stephens and McSween were old hands in the maintenance business and had a firm grip on the workforce; too firm at times.

Bill Taylor supervised the electrical and control staff. Bill had very good technicians who were quite familiar with programmable logic controllers and other types of control equipment.

Jerry Duffney supervised the Services group with trades such as Carpenter, insulator, labourer.

---

[44] By March 1984, the plant had produced 1250 tons of heavy water. Due to market conditions in 1984, production of heavy water was reduced by 54% relative to 1980. Total operating costs declined by 20% for the four-years 1980-1984, ending March 1984.

The Maintenance team overcame many obstacles over the years, including the heat exchanger corrosion problem. They took equipment apart and put it back together with great efficiency.

In 1979, or thereabouts, with the departure of Gerry Armitage as Production Manager and the subsequent restructuring of leadership roles, Arthur Pratt, accepted a position with the Saudi Arabian company, Aramco, in Yanbu, Saudi Arabia.[45]

Pratt's departure precipitated a search for a replacement. Following interviews, the choice came down to and older, experienced, manufacturing manager from Ontario and a 28-year-old engineer, born and raised in Newfoundland but currently living in British Columbia. The younger man came across as an energetic change agent which, at the time, the department needed. An offer was made and accepted and Derek Dymond was appointed Maintenance Manager.

Derek proved to be an outstanding manager. The plant benefited greatly from his leadership. He improved the capability and productivity of the maintenance department. His drive for continuous improvement sometimes got him into difficulty with the union. He made a very important contribution to the success of the plant[46].

Ben Cleary[47] joined the plant in the Production Department but was appointed Head of Planning, reporting to Derek Dymond. Ben

---

[45] Arthur was familiar with Saudi Arabia because he spent several years working there prior to joining AECL. He and his family were sad to give up a beautiful, forested property on Kings Road, overlooking Sydney Harbour. It subsequently became the site of a new motel.

[46] *Based on a Rollie story*: In the early months of Derek's tenure, I had occasion to walk with him through the maintenance shop. There was work going on in several areas of the shop. When we emerged, Derek gave me his impression of what he saw. Even while conversing with me, Derek had gathered information about all of the work that was under way and he described the work in impressive detail. He even noted the idle hands.

[47] Ben was a member of the plant's 'Newfie Mafia' which also included, Carl Taylor and Derek Dymond. It would have been hard to find three more capable people anywhere in Canada at that time. Each of them went on to career success in later years.

implemented a work order system that significantly improved the cost and effectiveness of our maintenance work.

In the early days, there was a lot of friction between Production and Maintenance. Production wants to 'produce', and this can wreak havoc on equipment, while Maintenance wants to 'maintain', and keep equipment in good repair. This conflict is brought into focus when equipment misbehaves and upsets the production process.

To correct the 'misbehavior' a work order is issued, usually by the Production Department. It is an 'order' to the Maintenance Department to do work on equipment. The work order specifies the equipment, the problem, and other relevant information. One of the important elements of the order is its Priority, that is, the importance and urgency of the work. In a 'sloppy' work order system most work orders are classified as Top Priority. This usually results in a breakdown of the system.

One of ways to test the effectiveness of a work order system is to compare the ratio of Top Priority with lower priorities, such as 'Low'. Top Priority work orders should not normally represent more than 20% of all work orders. Before Ben came along, 80% of the work orders were classified as Top Priority. In the absence of good planning, this creates havoc in the maintenance department.

In a well functioning planning system, Maintenance and Production discuss work orders daily and reach agreement as to the priority of each. Once agreed, the Planning group plan and schedule the work to be done. This means rationally scheduling time and resources for each work order.

Ben was a key player on the plant team. He had great judgement and he handled tough assignments very effectively. He was a straight shooter, respected by all who worked with him.

The Maintenance Engineering department was created in 1979. Howard McIntyre was Maintenance Engineering Superintendent. He had a small team consisting of two or three engineers and one or two technicians.

# ADMINISTRATION

Labor relations dominated the agenda of the Administration Department. Other important activities, were, plant security, medical clinic, public relations[48] and an extensive training effort. The department also managed a summer jobs program[49] for university students.

Bob Brown, an experienced labour relations negotiator, was Head of Administration. Bob left the plant in 1981 to accept a senior position at head office.

Denis Bouvette joined in 1976. He was an up and coming human resources manager and later had a very successful career with Bombardier.

Carl Taylor joined in 1980 and became Head of Administration a year or so later. Carl left the plant in 1986 following closure. His subsequent career led him into senior executive positions in labour relations and executive-level management in the food industry in Canada and the USA.

Donna Somerville initially worked in personnel records. Carl recruited her to assist him and in a relatively short time she became a Labour Relations specialist. Donna was an effective contributor to contract negotiations.

Support staff in the early days consisted of, Eleanor Gallant, Audrey Gouthro, Barbara MacDonald, Gordon [Turk] Stewart and Joe Poirier.

Bev MacIntosh was very effective in her role as plant nurse. She was smart and had a warm personality that put her 'patients' at ease.

---

[48] The plant operated a fully equipped public relations facility, on the other side of Glace Bay Lake, a few miles from the plant. This effort was part of AECL's overall public information program where the benefits of AECL's many nuclear energy projects and products were explained for the benefit of the public. The public relations program was the responsibility of David Morley.

[49] Summer Student Program - Employment opportunities for university students were few and far between in Cape Breton. Many plant employees had university-aged children and wanted them to have summer jobs to help defray the cost of university attendance. In the late 70s and into the 80s until plant closure, the plant operated a well-designed program for student summer jobs.

# SAFETY

The plant inherited a poor safety reputation from DCL that brought the plant under the microscope of the AECB and the Nova Scotia Dept. Of Labour. The December 1976 accident made things worse.

It was important to improve safety performance to the level of the other Canadian heavy water plants. The plant required better information on accidents. For example, lost time injury, frequency, severity, location, nature of the work, the work unit involved, the cost, e.g., workers compensation.

Close attention was paid to safety statistics and steps were taken and improve things. For example, if a work crew had a disproportionate number of accidents, a conversation with the work crew supervisor was required in which 'actions to improve' were discussed.

Two requirements of the AECB operating license were an Emergency Plan[50] and a Safety Manual. The Safety Manual covered all aspects of personnel safety, including protective equipment and the handling of hazardous substances. All staff were trained in safety procedures, particularly in the use of rescue breathing equipment.

In time, all employees bought into the importance of work place safety and developed a safe work culture. Some people might think that instilling the idea of 'safe work' is just an exercise in logic. To some extent it is, however there is an emotional and psychological component that builds

---

[50] The Emergency Plan included both plant and community components. If an incident at the plant posed a threat to the surrounding community, police, fire, medical and emergency teams would be notified immediately. Fortunately, this requirement ever arose. However, tests and training drills were held regularly to test the performance of safety systems. In the event of an emergency the Shift Supervisor was the person in charge. This was a heavy burden to carry, however, there was always a Manager on call who could be called out to assist. The key to an effective emergency response system was training, training, and more training. The emergency signals were tested each morning: *"Attention, Attention... This is a test of the plant emergency system."* Followed by the sound of the Alert, Emergency, and All Clear. Emergency crews were directed by a two-way radio from the Control Room.

commitment and excitement. The plant instituted a program of rewards for achievement of important safety goals, e.g., sports jackets, fire extinguishers, key fobs, alarm clocks, and other tangible gifts for safety achievements.

The plant had up to date equipment and trained staff to handle any foreseeable emergency. In addition to control room alarms and a public-address system, and many rescue stations strategically located around the plant site. A 'buddy' system ensured that no one worked alone in the gas containing units. A fire truck and an ambulance were available on a 24 x 7 basis with operating teams trained in their use.

An important health and safety asset was the Medical Clinic which was staffed with a full-time nurse, Bev McIntosh, who attended to the health needs of employees five days a week. On the off shifts, laboratory staff were trained in first aid and were available on a 24 x 7 basis. Employees were encouraged to check with the clinic for any health-related matters. A local doctor was engaged on contract and visited the plant regularly and was available for consultations on work-related injuries and rehabilitation.

Facilities and services are, in themselves, insufficient to ensure a safe workplace. Training programs, regular safety meetings, and other measures were aimed at ensuring awareness and understanding of the responsibility of each employee to undertake safe work.

From the late 1970s into the 1980s, until plant closure, thanks to the measures mentioned above, and with the understanding and cooperation of employees, plant safety improved to the credit of the employees.

In 1984, the plant celebrated a significant improvement in safety[51]. Record achievements in number of days worked without a lost time injury and other achievements for safe work. To celebrate, there was a buffet and dance for employees and spouses on Friday, May 3, 1985 at the Adult Vocational Training Centre on the Sydney-Glace Bay Highway, with music by Cheyenne and dancing until one AM.

---

[51] As of June 1984, 84 employees had worked more than 10 years and 161 work more than five years without a lost time accident. On July 6, 1984 a new Plant record of 124 continuous days with a lost time injury was achieved.

# STORES

Gerry Coleman was responsible for stores operation, assisted by Bill Singer. Maintenance of the plant required tools, equipment, and supplies of all kinds. This included spare parts for critical plant components such as pumps, valves, heat exchangers, gas blowers, piping and instrumentation. The plant also had a small fleet of transport and work equipment which required spark plugs, motor oil, filters, and other vehicle components. Stores also carried toilet paper, Kleenex, sanitary napkins, and a complete array of stationery supplies, pens, paper, paper clips, scotch tape, etc.

The plant had a cavernous warehouse with floor to ceiling shelves and an adjoining fenced area for storage of larger equipment, such as piping, large valves, heat exchanger tubes.

As cost saving became more important, the cost of operating stores came under the microscope. Month to month and year-over-year comparisons showed some interesting trends. For example, there was a large 'spike' in stationary consumption in late August. This was attributed to the 'back to school' demand as employees 'requisitioned' supplies for 'home use'. Vehicle maintenance parts and supplies were also being consumed at a rate far exceeding the needs of the small number of plant vehicles. 'Shrinkage', a euphemism for theft[52], was a problem that had to be solved. It wasn't major but was, nonetheless, a problem.

Plant vehicles were subject to search upon leaving the plant and some managers advocated instituting searches of departing employees during shift change. Van Alstyne didn't like the idea of subjecting employees to searches when only a small minority were responsible for theft.

As a result, 'attractive' items were identified, and it was decided not to keep them in plant stores. Instead, such items were obtained by local purchase order. These items received much more scrutiny with the result that 'shrinkage' was significantly reduced.

Since the plant possessed fully equipped workshops, and many employees were highly skilled tradesmen, a few employees worked on what were euphemistically called, 'government jobs'. These were personal projects assembled at the plant and then smuggled out. One of the methods

---

[52] Lest the reader get the impression that theft was rampant, GBHWP employees, were overwhelmingly honest and trustworthy.

used to smuggle projects, equipment and supplies was to toss them over the fence to recover it later. It was rumoured that several moonshine stills[53] were fabricated at the plant. To improve the overall security at the plant, chain-link fencing was reinforced, and lighting was improved.

---

[53] Cape Breton grew a reputation for its 'moonshine'. We're not talking about the evening glow of the Earth's moon, but the results of clandestine distillation of alcohol which produces its own unique 'glow'. It was rumoured that because the plant had excellent stainless-steel piping and other equipment suitable for construction as well as highly trained chemists and engineers, a few of Cape Breton's finest moonshine 'stills' were designed and built at the GBHWP. Another apocryphal story has a well-known moonshiner being confronted by the RCMP in the woods behind his home during the holiday season. He was carrying a 50-pound bag of sugar over his shoulder. When asked for an explanation he replied, "Nothing wrong with making a little bit of Christmas fudge, is there, officer?"

# UNIONS

Industrial Cape Breton has had an active union culture since the late 19th century. The coal miner's union was a social, cultural, and political force in Cape Breton with a long history of struggle in the face of mine safety concerns and the oppressive labour practices of the coal barons of the day.

In the early years of the 20$^{th}$ century, Governments were more sympathetic to the concerns of mine owners and often dispatched troops to quell labour unrest[54].

Glace Bay was a coal mining town dominated by the United Mineworkers. Steelworkers in nearby Sydney were also heavily unionized.

For decades, local politicians owed their success to the union vote. The arithmetic was persuasive, there were thousands of voters associated with unions and unions could get out the vote.

In a conflict with management, unions had the support of local politicians to leverage their point of view. As a Federal Crown Corporation, AECL was vulnerable to political leverage, especially when exercised at the Ministerial level. This was especially true in the politically charged environment of the heavy water industry in Cape Breton.

The Glace Bay plant had 3 unions. The Oil Chemical and Atomic Workers, [OCAW] represented two locals, the trades and operators, (all men), and a clerical union, (all women). ASEA, the technical/supervisory employees formed a third, unaffiliated, union local.

---

[54] Davis Day originated in memory of William Davis, a coal miner who was killed during a mining strike near the town of New Waterford. The protest was in response to a decision by the mining company, British Empire Steel and Coal Company, (BESCO), to shut down the drinking water supply and electricity to the town because of previous escalating strikes. Davis was shot and killed at approximately 11:00 AM on June 11, 1925 and many other miners were injured, when striking miners were charged by the company police force, whose officers fired over 300 shots. In the weeks and months following Davis' shooting, company facilities were looted and/or vandalized, despite the deployment of the provincial police force and 2,000 soldiers in what remains Canada's second-largest military deployment for an internal conflict, after the Northwest Rebellion.

An aggressive union culture influenced the heavy water plant unions in their approach to issues.

Plant supervisors and foremen made important contributions to the successful resolution of many labour relations issues. They were in the front lines and knew the people and the issues.

Contract negotiations with plant unions were conducted by plant managers but the position on important issues, such as money, was decided by head office. Since unionized employees at the Port Hawkesbury plant were represented by the same union some coordination was necessary.

The plant used the services of outside legal counsel in labor relations. This was particularly true in arbitration. A ringside seat during arbitration hearings revealed the skills of these very competent lawyers especially when they questioned witnesses[55].

The late John Kane was the OCAW Representative for Atlantic Canada.[56] John was a large man, with a pronounced Scottish accent. He sometimes came across as an old-style UK trade union militant, the kind that Maggie Thatcher often confronted. John communicated in pithy phrases like, "Let's stop sawing sawdust." The management side always volunteered to provide a printed version of the Union Agreement.[57]

---

[55] The plant was well served by lawyers Eric Durnford and Brian Johnston. Their successful track record meant that only important matters went to arbitration.

[56] In addition to John Kane, Local 785 was represented by its president, Art Fraser, and in earlier times by the then president, Ryan Sullivan. Union stewards, Francis Tighe and Gus Walsh were usually present.

[57] *A Rollie MacInnis Story*: At the conclusion of contract negotiations, Bob Brown volunteered to print copies of the collective agreement for both union and management. I suggested that we put a table of contents at the front and a keyword index at the back to make it easier to find things. Bob said that it was not in our interest to make it easier for union members to find clauses in the collective agreement. I've seen that 'let's not make it easy' principle applied in other situations over the years.

# EQUAL PAY

*A collective-bargaining two-step.*

In 1977, under pressure from lobby groups, Canada's Parliament inserted an equal-value theory into the Canadian Human Rights Act. It would now be a discriminatory practice for an employer to establish or maintain differences in wages between males and females employed in the same establishment and performing work of equal value. This is different from the principle of "equal pay for equal work," which has existed in Canada since the 1950s. Equal-work legislation made it illegal to pay different wages to men and women carrying out the same duties.

Equal value demands that men and women doing different jobs should be paid equally if those jobs have similar point scores after adding up the composite of skill, effort, responsibility and working conditions. Objections were raised arguing, for example, that the market conditions and collective bargaining should determine wages. The Act gave the Canadian Human Rights Commission a mandate to assess and investigate discrimination complaints to determine whether there was evidence of wage discrimination based on gender. If so determined, the complaint would be referred to a Canadian Human Rights Tribunal which could take steps to correct the apparent discrimination. Unions were quick to take advantage of this new workplace law.

The clerical union at the plant made a formal complaint to the Canadian Human Rights Commission arguing that their all-female bargaining group suffered sex discrimination in wages. The commission hired evaluation consultants who used a unique rubric to 'prove' that the jobs of clerks and tradesmen had similar point scores and should be paid the same, even though the market says you could hire a clerk for less than a tradesman. In other words, the commission found a way to equate an apple with an orange.

Because of the wide-ranging implications of this new union initiative, Doug Jordan, Marilyn Sykes and Bob Brown, from the Chemical Company Head Office, worked the issues and managed the file. Carl Taylor was the plant representative.

For the next two years, along with Lawyers, Eric Durnford and Brian Johnston, they worked this issue back and forth with the Union, the Commission and later with the Tribunal. There were many strategy sessions, job ranking reviews and hearings. The all-female union local stuck to their guns and, with a generalized feeling of injustice, pressed for a retroactive pay adjustment.

The AECL management team argued that the union had bargained, presumably in good faith, and had accepted their wages via contract. The tribunal ruled that notwithstanding the union's agreement, wage discrimination had occurred, and a retroactive pay adjustment was recommended.

In another twist, the Act prohibited achieving equity by cutting compensation. The result was a retroactive pay adjustment on top of wage gains the union had already bargained and agreed to.

The case went on for years and was forced to a conclusion by plant closure. Carl Taylor presented the 'final' offer of settlement. Carl said that with the plant closure announcement, it was the union's last chance to resolve the case since there was a tribunal hearing scheduled for the next day. Carl said that if there was no deal, management's settlement offer would be taken off the table. The National union representative accepted the offer and petitioned the CHRC to drop the case because agreement had been reached. The members of the all-female union received a retroactive compensation adjustment.

John Kane was not party to the final negotiations and he disagreed with his National union. He tried to carry on at the tribunal without the plaintiff but was rebuffed. The CHRC accepted the agreement and the case was resolved and closed.

Equal value proved a difficult idea to implement and changes were made in 2017 after the Federal Government spent $4 billion in retroactive pay adjustments for federal public servants. Public-sector pay equity was returned to the collective bargaining table and new legislation required the Commission to take market forces into account.

This ended the collective-bargaining two-step that encouraged public-sector unions to ask the Canadian Human Rights Commission to adjust wages already agreed to[58].

---

[58] Another bad idea: equal pay for work of equal value: Tom Flanagan, Globe and Mail, February 24, 2009, Updated March 27, 2017.

# UNITED WAY GOLD

Given the checkered history of the plant, it was important to establish the plant's *bona fides* with surrounding communities. Employees were encouraged to join a community service organization and the plant supported them with, recognition, time off and other forms of encouragement.

One of the important achievements[59] was the Cape Breton County United Way Gold award. Workers raised $11,000 through payroll deductions, $1000 over the goal. The gold award was based on a minimum 50% employee participation and a $50 per donor average. Heavy water employees exceeded both criteria. United Way Campaign Chairman Joyce McDougall expressed hope that other companies would follow the plant's example. The contribution of over $11,000 demonstrated a continuing commitment to the welfare of the communities and to the United Way.

---

[59] Campaign leaders were: George Karaphillis, George Stoliar, Trudy Mac Donald, Augustine [Gus] Walsh.

# COMPENSATION AND DISABILITY

One worrisome element of the health and safety program was the extraordinary uptake of Workers Compensation[60] and Disability[61]. Sometimes, perceived abuse led to union-management conflict.

The safety record at DEVCO[62] was abysmal. In the 1980s, DEVCO had about 10% of its workforce 'on the comp'. Being 'on the comp' was perhaps considered a benefit. Coal mining is inherently dangerous. Statistically speaking, in the 1980s, working for two weeks in a coal mining presented a one-in-a-million chance of dying!

Heavy water plant safety performance was closely tied to the Canadian Nuclear Industry where safety was a top priority. Canada's nuclear plants worked millions of man-hours without a lost time injury.

Opponents of nuclear power liked nothing better than to characterize nuclear power as inherently dangerous. Thus, the industry was determined to be as safe as it could be.

An interesting feature of the Workers Compensation Program in Nova Scotia was that, for Federal Crown Corporations, e.g., DEVCO, AECL, the entire cost of compensation was paid from the federal, not provincial, coffers. Nova Scotia administered the program. Thus, it cost the provincial treasury next to nothing. Without casting aspersions on how the province administered this program, there seemed to be little incentive for them to worry about cost.

In the early days of AECL's operation, the number of employees on Workers Compensation was disproportionately large, as was the cost when compared to other heavy water plants.

To mitigate these extraordinary costs, a 'light duties' program was introduced for employees injured on the job and yet capable of doing some

---

[60] Workers Compensation is an insurance program whereby an employee injured on the job continues to receive salary while off the job and recovering.

[61] Long Term Disability [LTD] kicks in when an employee on regular sick leave requires longer term care.

[62] The Cape Breton Development Corporation [DEVCO], a federal Crown Corporation, assumed responsibility for the coal mines as part of an overall program of industrial development in Cape Breton.

'light duties' work. For example, a mechanic who injured a finger might be assigned to the tool crib for a week or two while the finger healed. Tool crib duty consisted of dispensing and receiving specialized tools used in the plant, not a physically demanding job.

The plant nurse, Bev McIntosh, sometimes visited the homes of injured workers to check on their recovery and to ensure that they were following doctor's orders. This practice brought about some union resistance.

# INFORMATION SYSTEM

Plant financial and payroll information was keyed in at the plant but kept in AECL's Head Office on a mainframe. Desktop and other forms of 'localized' information management had yet to appear. The desktop computer and the VisiCalc spreadsheet were a 1980s thing. Home computers with a whopping 640k of storage cost $3000 and nine-pin tractor-fed printers cost $2000.

AECL's monthly 'dump' of hundreds of pages of tractor-feed computer output was painful to wade through and was marginally useful. It was like steering a car by the rear-view mirror.

The dynamics of managing the plant depended upon useful databases, operator instinct and good judgement. Management was primarily a control, planning and response function.

An important consideration in the early application of computers to management decision-making was the cost and complexity of mainframes. The day-to-day problems of an operating plant weren't of sufficient importance to chew up valuable mainframe time...except for evaluating whether to close the plant...a story that comes later in this book.

The emergence of the minicomputer and desktop computing changed this 'top-down' approach and enabled a localized approach to using information. For a fraction of the cost of a mainframe, a plant, could install and program a minicomputer to effect better operating decisions.

GBHWP took advantage of this emerging trend and, thanks to some deft manipulation of the budget and a liberal interpretation of the purchasing rules, a minicomputer was purchased, programmed, and installed.

Experience in programming a minicomputer was a vital consideration and fortunately George Karaphillis, a bright plant engineer, had such experience and he led a small team in the development of plant applications.

A team of information 'users' was assembled to identify specific information needs and assist Karaphillis in setting up the new minicomputer. Several important applications were developed.

One of the most important applications was a Maintenance Work Order System to enable the maintenance department to plan and schedule their work. A Work Order System is taken for granted in most plants today, but it was not back then. It was an innovative approach in its day.

Prior to computerization of maintenance work, it was a major challenge to decide the priority of work and to schedule its implementation. Resources such as manpower and equipment cost money. Every production operator who issued a work order thought that his work was the most important and should be undertaken immediately. Often this meant scheduling overtime and deployment of expensive, often rented, maintenance equipment. In effect, it was difficult to control the cost of maintenance. Computerization of maintenance work did not solve all the problems, but it went a long way towards a more rational and cost-effective approach.

We were assisted in this work by a St. Francis Xavier University Professor, Dr. Kent Young. His experience and understanding of information system proved invaluable. There were, however, occasions when academic freedom had to give way to operational necessity.

Thanks to better decision-making tools the production cost of heavy water gradually came down as production efficiency improved.

# GREENHOUSE

Hundreds of thousands of gallons of fresh water originating in McAskill's Brook flowed through the plant each day. Some of it yielded the heavy water product but most of it was used for cooling the equipment. There were strict regulations regarding the quality and temperature of water returned to Glace Bay Lake and, eventually, to the Atlantic Ocean. The temperature of the water was reduced to an acceptable level by giant cooling towers[63] and an extensive effluent channel with cooling water sprays.

In 1981[64] it was decided that, as an experimental project, some of the warm water discharged from the plant would be used in a greenhouse operation. A greenhouse was erected adjacent to the plant and used hydroponic[65] methods to grow cucumbers and tomatoes.

---

[63] Anti-nuclear protesters sometimes mistake cooling tower evaporation at nuclear plants for radioactive discharge. Most video news reports critical of the nuclear industry will feature harmless clouds of water vapour rising from cooling towers to play on this misunderstanding.

[64] Cape Breton Post March 30, 1981. An interesting project has been the establishment of a demonstration greenhouse on land adjacent to the plant a joint project of five levels of government including the Department of regional economic expansion, Atomic Energy of Canada Limited Chemical Company, Cape Breton development Corporation, and Nova Scotia Department of Mines and Energy and Agriculture. This project will identify an attempt to resolve the engineering difficulties encountered in the operation of such of facilities. Secondly, the greenhouse operations will attempt to establish the economic viability of growing tomatoes and cucumbers utilizing the thermal effluent discharge from the plant. The Glace Bay heavy water plant provides engineering assistance, freshwater, thermal affluent and security services to the greenhouse project.

[65] The project was technically successful and proved the concept. Imminent plant closure curtailed further development. tomatoes. Demand exceeded supply as local merchants valued the produce and plant employees purchased tomatoes as well.

# THE HANDWRITING

Through 1984 and into 1985, a staccato stream of 'do and don't' instructions were issued to managers of the Cape Breton plants.

AECL's Cape Breton employees were aware of the rumour mill and the frequent speculations of national and regional news media.

People were nervous and worried. Hardly a day went by when, yet another union representative or employee confronted a plant manager with questions about the future.

Questions such as, "I'm thinking about buying a new car, would you recommend that I do?"

Livelihoods and settled family life was at risk. The plant's future looked dim, if not yet fully decided, and yet managers dared not speculate as to what the future might bring except with their closest confidants.

There was to be no changes in employment, production levels, purchases, or anything that might 'signal' what everyone knew. Nonetheless, plant production was cut back, and energy money saved, under the guise of improving efficiency and productivity. What conscientious manager could continue to burn money in an apparently lost cause?

Arrangements were made with the local Community College to provide a training program for Control Technicians. Thus, instead of 'layoff' the head count of Control Technicians was reduced by half by sending some back to school. This was a 'win-win' situation since control technicians were better prepared for good jobs following plant closure. As it turned out, this was a very wise decision. Following closure, Ford of Canada offered a job in Windsor, Ontario to every Glace Bay Control Technician. A few took them up on their offer.

The handwriting was on the wall, the plants would be closed.

# THE FOUNTAIN OF WISDOM

*The words of a man's mouth are deep waters; the fountain of wisdom is a bubbling brook. - Proverbs 18:4*

Largely unknown to the people at the Cape Breton plants, the top decision makers in Ottawa[66] were concerned about the growing surplus of heavy water at Canadian plants in the face of a bleak forecast of CANDU reactor sales. The Heavy Water Projects team in Ottawa busied themselves with computer generated supply and demand scenarios.

The 'parent' ministry of AECL was the Energy Mines and Resources Department, EM&R. Both AECL and Ontario Hydro received strong political support from federal and provincial governments throughout the 1960s and into the 1970s[67].

The DCL fiasco and other early setbacks in the heavy water program, brought both AECL and EM&R under the microscope of the Prime Minister's Office, PMO, and the skeptical assessment of the powerful Privy Council Office, PCO.[68] The staff at EM&R relied on the Heavy Water Projects team to inform them about heavy water supply and demand.

Insofar as the Cape Breton plant were concerned, the Heavy Water Projects assessment and recommendations of supply and demand was worrisome in itself. Simply put, there was too much heavy water being supplied to meet too little demand and, consequently, Canadian heavy water plants would have to be shut down.

A Cabinet Memorandum was prepared. It recommended stopping construction of LaPrade and questioned the merits of future heavy water

---

[66] Heavy Water Projects, led by Al Dahlinger, AECL's Corporate Office, led by AECL, CEO, Jim Donnelly.

[67] Prime Minister Jean Chretien was an exceptionally strong advocate of Canada's CANDU Program.

[68] The Privy Council Office, PCO, is the Secretariat of the Federal Cabinet of Canada, which is a committee of the Queens Privy Counsel for Canada. The PCO provides non-partisan advice and support to Canadian ministries, as well as leadership, coordination, and support to departments and agencies of government. The Office of the Prime Minister [PMO] is one of the most powerful parts of the government.

production by AECL. The situation was characterized by volatile politics, hard-core engineering, and mathematics. Nonetheless, very senior people in government relied on the results. A 150-page Cabinet Memorandum document was completed and delivered to the PCO. The Heavy Water Projects estimate of supply and demand was the 'kiss of death' for LaPrade, Glace Bay and Port Hawkesbury. The purported reason that plant production carried on for several more years was that a Canadian Strategic Reserve was added to the demand forecast. This latter development might also have been a political decision, simply to buy time.

# THE ELEPHANT

It was hard to ignore the 'elephant in the room' trumpeting plant closure. In 1983 the plant lowered costs rather than increase production. In 1984, the emphasis shifted to lowering production levels to save money. Production units were sometimes idled.

Because of efficiencies gained and lower production levels, there were more employees than necessary and one of the most obvious ways to "save money" was to reduce head count via layoffs. However, the plants were instructed not to implement a layoff.

Plant employees were aware of the rumour mill, and the endless speculation of national and regional news media. Hardly a day went by when one or another union representative or employee confronted a manager or supervisor with a question about the future of the plant. Employees were understandably nervous because their livelihoods and family life was at risk. Plant managers knew that the plant's future was dim, if not fully decided, and yet were instructed not to speculate as to what the future might bring. They wanted to prepare employees for change and new jobs, probably elsewhere.

Anyone with half a brain knew that the handwriting was on the wall. The plants would be closed. Plant managers danced around the issue for a year or more in a Cape Breton version of Fantasia.

With the benefit of 20-20 hindsight, a plant born in the hands of political midwives would die at the hands of a political undertakers.

The elephant was symbolized in other ways as well. It served as a humorous beginning to slide presentations on heavy water production. Just below the bold title HEAVY WATER? there was a photo of a huge squatting elephant having a gushing pee. It always got a laugh. In a few editorial cartoons a white elephant was depicted as a way of poking fun at the plant.

# STRIKING SYMBOLS

On May 23, 1985, Finance Minister, Hon. Michael Wilson presented his first budget[69]. Anticipating the worst, the management team watched Wilson's presentation in a conference room at the plant. Most employees watched at home.

Wilson had Cape Breton's heavy water plants in his political crosshairs and he announced closure with these words...

*"The heavy water plants in Glace Bay and Port Hawkesbury are recognized as striking symbols of government waste and mismanagement. They cost the taxpayers of this country more than $100 million per year to produce a product for which there is no demand. We will move immediately to close the plants, but we will not abandon the people or the region of Cape Breton. Workers at the plants will receive generous*

---

[69] Wilson Budget Note, 1985.Continued operation of AECL's two heavy water plants on Cape Breton Island can no longer be justified. There are ample supplies of heavy water already on hand and alternative sources are available to cover all foreseeable domestic and export requirements. The operation of both plants has been fully funded by the government since 1981; funding requirements for 1985-86 were projected at $115 million. Once plant closures have been carried out, it is anticipated that savings will exceed $100 million annually. Workers will be provided with generous severance benefits, retraining and relocation assistance and financial and career counselling, together with measures designed to facilitate re-employment. The impact on the affected communities' property tax revenues will also be offset for a period. As part of the budget, a special tax credit will be introduced to enhance private sector investment and productive employment on Cape Breton Island. More details are provided in Section I of the Budget Papers. In addition, a private sector Advisory Committee will be asked to review development opportunities and advise within a few months on special Cape Breton development measures that may warrant federal support. Details will be announced shortly on AECL's heavy water plant closures and adjustment plans and on the government's Cape Breton regional development effort, including the approval process for the special tax credit and the Advisory Committee's membership and terms of reference.

*severance benefits and will be assisted in seeking new employment.*
*Atomic Energy of Canada Limited will be announcing further details of*
*these measures shortly. "*

The announcement was punctuated by a collective groan within the group. It was intensely personal. How could Wilson's characterization of years of hard work and dedication by well educated, competent people be characterized as, *'striking symbols of government waste and mismanagement'*? It seemed an unnecessary kick in the groin. One wondered, "What aspiring political hack penned those words?"

To be fair, those words were probably aimed at Pierre Trudeau, Alan J. McEachen and the recently defeated Liberal government and not at the employees of the plants themselves. However, such political warfare was lost on employees. No cabinet minister was about to lose his job…at least not then. Politicians care mostly about power; how to get it, how to use it, how to keep it. You see this in the headlines every day.

The Mulroney government was elected on a promise to clean house, cut spending, and issue 'pink slips and running shoes' to public servants. Most Canadians voted to end Liberal Government rule and supported Wilson's characterization of the Cape Breton heavy water plants. Above all, Mulroney's PC government seemed determined to erase the legacy of Alan J. McEachen. The Tories never forgot McEachern's behind-the-scenes engineering of the demise of the Joe Clark Government in 1979.

Some Canadians of the day had a decidedly negative view of Cape Breton, its workers, and the hundreds of millions of dollars spent on failed attempts to lift the island out of its seemingly perpetual economic distress.

In fairness to AECL and the Mulroney government, plant employees were treated fairly and generously, notwithstanding their need to search far and wide for employment. Most employees remained in Cape Breton to look for work and a few decided to start new businesses. Some moved away to find employment elsewhere. Skilled employees had no difficulty in securing jobs in places like Fort McMurray, Alberta.

Closure of Cape Breton's heavy water plants meant the loss of a $100 million/year industry, a significant blow to an island of 150 thousand people. Hundreds of millions of dollars were spent on coal-fired steam provided by Nova Scotia Power via coal from DEVCO. A blow of this magnitude would be the equivalent of losing a $10 billion industry in Toronto in 2018, roughly equivalent to losing the Royal Bank of Canada.

# CLOSURE

The light at the end of the tunnel was out.

Prior to its presentation to Canada's Parliament, the federal budget is a secret document. Thus there was no advance warning of heavy water plant closure. To be fair the signs were there, months, if not years, beforehand. Some Glace Bay employees departed before Wilson's closure announcement. Derek Dymond accepted a position with AECL's Radiochemical Company and left early in 1985. His departure required changes in the top team. Derrick Aucoin was appointed Maintenance Manager, Garth Spinney was appointed Production Manager and Adrian White was appointed Technical Manager. This was the first wave in a year of dizzying change. A plant closure announcement was posted[70] and plans long since hidden in desk drawers were dusted off. These plans covered how layoffs would occur, what compensation would be given to employees, and what support would be provided to help employees find

---

[70] ATOMIC ENERGY OF CANADA LIMITED, CANDU OPERATIONS, GLACE BAY HEAVY WATER PLANT, PLANT NOTICE, PLANT CLOSURE

Last night the Finance Minister announced the permanent closure of both the Glace Bay and Port Hawkesbury Heavy Water Plants. I regret the fact that you got such important information directly from the media and not from AECL first.

For the time being, operations will continue while plans are detailed for a safe and orderly shutdown. The Glace Bay plant will probably cease production in the next few weeks after which hydrogen sulfide and other chemicals will be removed, and the equipment will be cleaned for disassembly and disposal. Layoffs will occur as work is completed to the limits of approved funding levels.

There will be discussions with Union officers and other employees as plans are finalized. The assistance plans will be outlined to you at meetings to be held next week. We must now work together during this difficult period and ensure that we follow plant rules and procedures to ensure safe conclusion for work in the months ahead.- Signed: Rollie MacInnis, General Manager 1985 May 24.

other jobs and, if necessary, relocate[71]. Employee options were split between those willing to leave to find other opportunities and those who clung tenaciously to the land of their birth. Closing the plant was not as simple as turning off a light switch since the plant contained hundreds of tons of toxic gas that had to be dealt with. Over the next few months, operating units were shut down, cleaned and mothballed. When the wind direction was favourable, blowing out over the ocean with sufficient force to disperse the products of combustion, hydrogen sulphide gas was burned off. Thus, the last vestiges of operational life were removed. A decision on final disposition of the plant was expected within two years.

The announcement of closure produced an avalanche of media reports. Many reports were aired before AECL had an opportunity to fully disclose its plans to employees. Reports characterized employees reaction as "shocked and angry" at the loss of 700 plant jobs and a further 1000 jobs in support industries. Reporters pursued employees through plant parking lots and shoved microphones in their faces. They asked questions like, "What are you planning to do now that you're out of work?" Employees with bowed heads mumbled phrases like, "I'll find something I hope." A few employees said they expected closure and said that they were not surprised. Reporters, standing with the now dead plant in the background, traced plant history and emphasized that heavy water demand had dried up and AECL stockpiled heavy water at a cost of $100 million.

Glace Bay union representatives accepted what was described as a "most generous severance package" comparable to the package offered to Iron Ore Company of Canada [IOC] employees when Brian Mulroney, then President of IOC, closed IOC's Schefferville plant in 1981[72].

---

[71] The human resources consulting firm of Robertson, Surette, located in Halifax, provided the plant with an excellent manual on relocation counselling.

[72] The loss of 1700 jobs at Schefferville could have been the end of Mulroney's political career. In a 1977 interview with the CBC, Mulroney vowed he would never run again for the Tory leadership saying: "I wouldn't touch it with a 10-foot pole." However, Mulroney's astute handling of the Schefferville situation propelled him back onto the public stage and led eventually to his election as Prime Minister. Obviously in the intervening years he managed to whittle a 20-foot pole.

Within days of closure, a press conference was held in Sydney where Hugh Van Alstyne, AECL V.P., explained the closure process. He was accompanied by Rollie MacInnis, Glace Bay Manager, [the author of this book], and Roger Jeffries, Port Hawkesbury Manager. Van Alstyne said the plant would be protected for an indefinite period to render it physically safe for employees and the public.

The press conference was attended by several dour-faced union representatives accompanied by John Kane, National Rep. For the OCAW.

Job search expenses were to be paid, and employee houses were to be purchased by AECL. Workers received twice the normal severance pay.

Much later, under pressure from unions and politicians, AECL reluctantly agreed to divide the proceeds of housing sales among those employees who remained in Cape Breton. There was no precedent for this degree of generosity and some AECL Board Members were opposed to this gesture.

Michael Wilson, Minister of finance, was interviewed via CBC Halifax. He was asked whether he thought the closure and layoffs were 'fair'. His response was that 'everyone knew' the plants were losing money for years and the product had no market, so it was just a question of time as to when closure would happen. In recognition of the economic situation of Cape Breton Island, Wilson announced new tax initiatives to encourage investment on Cape Breton Island.

Jim Donnelly, AECL President, released details of the severance offer at a meeting of the Natural Resources and Public Works Standing Committee. he described the package as "very generous" and said it met the "highest standards".

# TERMS OF TERMINATION

*Two leaps per chasm is fatal*
*– Chinese proverb.*

Shortly after the announcement of closure a committee representing employees and management was convened to negotiate severance[73]. Port Hawkesbury and Glacé Bay plants aimed to synchronize their respective meetings to avoid conflicts.

At first, employees were lukewarm to the adjustment proposals put forth by management. While there was general agreement, there was a major sticking point in how employees hired from outside Cape Breton, i.e. CFA', [Come from Away], were treated versus the local population, RCB, [Real Cape Bretoners].

The agreement provided job search services, relocation assistance, house purchases and paid trips for job interviews. Charlie MacDonald argued from the perspective of the RCB employees that this constituted inequitable treatment since many RCB employees simply did not want to relocate. By MacDonald's logic, CFA's received a financial benefit although they were simply being repaid for expenses they incurred in their job search and relocation.

The management team was surprised by this 'logic'. Carl Taylor argued that relocating a family and starting a new job did not constitute a 'financial benefit'. On the contrary, it was a huge disruption. This so-called benefit was available to anyone who wanted to take advantage of it. Adjustment wasn't a zero-sum game. Legitimate expenses paid to those who wanted to leave didn't somehow create a disadvantage for those who wanted to stay. Charlie was adamant that it constituted a benefit to those who would be leaving vs. those who wanted to stay.

Maintaining a consistent management position with employees at each plant, i.e. Port Hawkesbury and Glace Bay, was a major challenge since each plant had its own adjustment committee and conducted independent

---

[73] Federally regulated employers, such as AECL, when planning a group termination must establish a committee of employer and employee representatives to develop an adjustment program immediately upon delivering a notice of group termination.

negotiations. John Kane and the unionized employees of the ECW recognized this problem and played both sides to advantage.

The actions of AECL executives in relation to the closure of the Cape Breton plants came under scrutiny by politicians of all stripes.

AECL's president, Jim Donnelly, paid a visit the plant in the early stages of closure and layoffs. He met with the management team and wanted to know who was leading the discussion with employees. Carl Taylor was identified, and Donnelly turned to him and wanted to know what was going on. Carl gave a summary of closure discussions and he identified an impasse over the treatment of those staying versus those leaving. Donnelly said that he had politicians and unions running around Ottawa demanding a better deal and he was fed up with the whole process. He wanted the impasse resolved and said something to the effect, "I want you to paint the sky blue, but don't spend any more money."

Donnelly's statement put Carl in a very difficult position, the proverbial rock and hard place scenario. When Carl left the meeting, he began a round of discussions with Doug Jordan's HR team in Ottawa. Doug, Marilyn Sykes, and Bob Brown put their heads together and came up with a new idea that would not cost any more money.

The essence of the idea was to redistribute monies received from the sale of AECL-purchased houses. These houses had been purchased by AECL from employees who left Cape Breton to find jobs elsewhere. These houses were subsequently sold, some at bargain basement prices. It was a novel idea and was in the words of some, 'a big giveaway'. However, it was an easy proposition to redirect existing AECL money then to ask the government for more.

That afternoon, Carl presented the new proposal to employees on the adjustment committee. He began by discussing the trust fund to be set up to distribute the proceeds of house sales to those deciding to remain in Cape Breton. There was widespread support for this compromise. Carl said that the company was prepared to pay each remaining employee a bonus if everything was agreed unanimously. Charlie McDonald asked for a caucus and they returned in less than five minutes to support the proposal. The deal was done in less than two hours. The final language of the deal was written up and signed within 24 hours.

Later, the Port Hawkesbury team ran into problems but following consultations with Glace Bay and the Ottawa office, an agreement was eventually reached.

Severance payments to employees were essentially the same for union and non-union employees. In the case of unionized employees, layoffs followed the seniority list as defined in union contracts. Layoffs were done in stages, as operating condition permitted. Some maintenance activities continued in accordance with plans to clean and preserve the equipment.

Human resources staff geared up to help employees during this difficult transition. The plant offered training in job search techniques resume writing and other aids to finding new employment. The plant contacted potential employers across Canada and offered to pay them for recruiting trips to the plant. Ford Motor Company, based in Windsor, Ontario and Syncrude, based in Fort McMurray, Alberta took advantage of this offer and came to the plant for interviews. Several employees gained new jobs that way. Such efforts were 'leading edge' initiatives in employee adjustment at that time.

As a goodwill gesture, when the H2S was removed, Van Alstyne authorized distribution of safety and emergency equipment to local fire and emergency departments.

VanAlstyne was also concerned with older non-union workers, I.e., those over 55 years of age, who were less than two years away from pensionable service. Some were offered employment as non-union security staff until their pension eligibility kicked in, at which time they were laid off.

One of the major challenges faced by an operating plant during closure is the need to retain key staff to ensure a safe and orderly transition. This is especially true of an operating heavy water plant.

In the months prior to the closure announcement, key employees were offered and accepted financial incentives to remain with the plant until their services were no longer required. Once released, they faced the same uncertainty as everyone else, finding a job, relocating families to new communities, spousal unemployment, settling in.

# DISPERSED AND DISMANTLED

In the latter half of 1985 and into 1986, the ranks of employees thinned until only security guards were left on the plant site.

Employees dispersed; across Canada, into the United States and overseas. Many employees remained in Cape Breton. Some have maintained close contact during the thirty plus years since the plant closed. Some created successful businesses in Cape Breton: Fred Hill, George Karaphillis, Billy McMullin, Shelly Brown, Jim O'Handley, Bev MacIntosh. One or two had misadventures[74].

Soon after closure, it was decided to dismantle the plant. Equipment such as pumps, motors, valves, instrumentation was recovered and sold to interested bidders. Towers, piping, vessels, and steel structures were demolished and sold for scrap. The gigantic GS towers were felled in the same manner used to demolish buildings. Explosive charges were set around the circumference of the base and detonated. The towers shook and gradually toppled, one by one, hitting the ground with a colossal 'whump' raising gigantic clouds of dust, and debris.

What remained of this vibrant plant, once humming with activity, were a few large buildings and concrete foundations surrounded by a chain-link fence.

The Public Relations Building and function was closed a year before closure of the plant. Dave Morley, 'PR guy', was laid off at that time.

---

[74] One of the more colourful characters at the plant, Larry Shanahan, got into trouble with the law and in 2006 was sent to prison for 2 1/2 years. In July 2004 he walked into a packed union meeting of the International Brotherhood of Electrical Workers in Whitney Pier and pointed a gun at a fellow union member. He was originally charged with attempted murder, but charges were downgraded when he agreed to plead guilty to lesser charges. He was ordered to continue counselling in prison for alcoholism and anger management. problems and was obliged to submit a DNA sample to the national registry. A 10-year weapons ban was also imposed. Long after the plant closed, it was rumoured that while working the night shift, Larry had walked naked around the plant wearing only his protective breathing equipment.

AECL entered a memorandum of understanding with Enterprise Cape Breton, ECB, whereby ECB would oversee remediation and final disposition of the plant site.

According to the annual report of 1988 – 1989, AECL wrote off an $800 million investment in the three heavy water plants, Glace Bay, Port Hawkesbury, LaPrade.

# DEMOLITION

*From World Centre to Eyesore- Cape Breton Post, December 1963.*
*A long-time eyesore on the outskirts of Glace Bay. CBC May 2013*

The plant, conceived as a 'world center' in 1963, was fifty years later, an 'eyesore'. Twenty-seven years passed since closure and the remaining plant buildings stood mostly vacant. Over its fifty-year life span, the plant had a productive life of about eight years. The remaining forty-two years was spent in conception, construction, reconstruction, rehabilitation, demolition, argument and idleness. In the spring of 2013, excavators began tearing down and exhuming the concrete remains of the plant.

AECL retained the firm of Greenspoon Bros[75] Demolition, of Toronto, to dismantle the plant. Local 785 claimed the right to do the dismantling work and filed a grievance. The basis of their claim was that they had maintained the equipment and were best qualified to dismantle it. The grievance ended up in the hands of an arbitrator. Ira Greenspoon, the CEO of Greenspoon Bros., attended the arbitration meetings the union could not figure out who he was. Some suspected he was from the Employment Agency to check if people were double dipping. AECL's lawyer, Eric Durnford did a masterful job of presenting management's position to the arbitrator. He called upon Ira Greenspoon and Derrick Aucoin to say that demolition is very different work than maintenance of an operating plant, arguing that safety was the top priority. It was a persuasive argument and the arbitrator ruled in favour of AECL.

In 2012, several boarded-up buildings and a tangle of underground pipes and concrete remained at the site. Eight of the remaining buildings were torn down in December of 2012.

---

[75] In what was perhaps an ironic twist of fate, Greenspoon Bros. Ltd. a third-generation company went bankrupt in April of 2003. The company had been in business for 70 years and made their living demolishing other people's buildings. In addition to demolition of the heavy water plants, it levelled Toronto's Exhibition Stadium, the former home of the Toronto Blue Jays; the former Via railway station in London, Ont., and the old Victory Soya Mills site on Toronto's harbourfront. Mr. Greenspoon said one of his biggest kicks came from fulfilling every school kid's fantasy. "We actually tore down a school I went to."

What remained to be done in the spring of 2013 was concrete demolition, some building demolition, recovering for recycling and moving soils.

Enterprise Cape Breton Corporation, owners of the site by agreement with AECL, wanted to rehabilitate the property to make it suitable for residential and/or commercial use. Some 50,000 tons of concrete was removed as well as some heavy metals and some hydrocarbons.

Because the property bordered the shoreline of Glace Bay Lake, special precautions were needed to protect the environment. Remediation of the site was completed in 2014 and the $3,000,000 cost was paid by the federal government. The Cape Breton Regional Municipality is now in the process of rezoning the 150-hectare site. Occasionally, a former employee will pass by the site and remember[76].

---

[76] I pass the Heavy Water property several times a week. Hard to believe it is now nothing more than a dog walking track! We had so many good times there. We all still refer to it as the best job we ever had. Our little group, (Joan Corbett, Debbie Calabrese, Debbie MacIntyre, and Chris Gallant), meet regularly and often reminisce about all the fun we had. We always managed to get the work done. Not too long ago, I ran across copies of some of the cartoons that circulated at the plant - so many good memories. - Betty Rankin – April 2018

# REUNION 2001

Canadian East Coast culture fosters strong family and social relationships. These relationships infuse workplaces. Cape Breton's coal mines, steel plant, colleges, schools, and other workplaces were hotbeds of humour and camaraderie. Many employees socialized with coworkers outside of the workplace in curling clubs, bowling leagues, roller skating, swimming, hunting and fishing expeditions, ball teams, hockey teams, bridge clubs, tarabish clubs, ceilidhs, kitchen parties, and the many other ways in which East Coast people enjoy their lives within communities.

In 2001, 16 years after closure, a dedicated group of former employees decided that a Glace Bay Heavy Water Plant Reunion was long overdue. Francis Sampson, Joan Corbett, Jim O Handley, Bev McIntosh, Chris Gallant, Ron Evely, Debbie McIntyre, and Larry Johnson organized the first and only reunion of former plant employees.

On the evening of August 24, 2001, a hundred or more-people gathered at the Nova Scotia Community College, Marconi campus, on the Sydney-Glace Bay Highway. There was a lottery draw for gifts provided by local businesses and former employees. The large room had cafeteria seating and was decorated with garlands. A large "Welcome" sign was hung just behind the main stage. There was food and drink for everyone and from the start it was obvious that people would have fun and enjoy the opportunity to share memories of a past life and to catch up on current events.

Everyone received an 80-page brochure with coloured pictures of the plant, newspaper clippings, newspaper cartoons, poems, songs and stories about the plant's history. The brochure also contained photos of employees during important moments in the history of the plant such as the first drum of heavy water.

Some of the most memorable moments at the GBHWP during the AECL Years were captured in Ron Evely cartoons. The brochure contained many of his depictions of life at the plant. Ron had an eye for character and events and created uncanny images of his fellow employees in all kinds of situations. Whether he was caricaturing Art Pratt in Saudi Arabia, Leroy Petrie in tennis garb, Ben Cleary in an embarrassing sailing accident, Bruce Addicott's Dalhousie jacket, Bobby Fraser using the women's washroom, hockey incidents, Gerry Armitage nativity scenes, poking fun at managers and supervisors, or mocking Local 785's union executive, he skillfully and humorously captured many plant events. Hats off to Ron! The organizing committee greeted everyone. Chris Gallant was determined to get a photograph of every person in attendance. At one point in the evening the entire production team was assembled onstage for photographs. This group included shift supervisors and foremen as well as many of the operating crew. The management team was represented by: Hugh Van Alstyne, Gerry Armitage, Carl Taylor, Bob Brown, Rollie MacInnis.

The event was very well received by all those in attendance and for many it represented a unique opportunity to renew friendships. Many employees have kept in touch to this very day.

# APPENDIX 1 - STORIES

## TIM ANDREEFF

### DCL RECRUITING

## Based on a Tim Andreeff Story

It was midmorning on a cool February day in 1968. Light snow frosted the sidewalks of Kings College Road on the campus of the University of Toronto.

The Technical Manager at DCL, stepped through the front door of the Engineering Annex, brushed snow from his boots, approached the receptionist's desk, and asked for directions to meeting room 2C. The gray-haired receptionist wordlessly jabbed her pencil straight up. He assumed she meant the second floor.

U of T was his first stop on his Ontario University recruiting trip. He hoped to recruit newly graduated engineers to help his technical team commission Jerome Spevack's heavy water plant. The University of Toronto promised top talent and he had lined up interviews with Tim and Paul, two promising candidates. He figured it would be a challenge to convince these young engineers, used to big city life, to take a chance on his plant and life in a small coal-mining town.

He was early and when he entered room 2C he settled into a sturdy oak chair behind a single-pedestal desk with a laminated top. He rummaged in his briefcase, removed his notebook and files, and prepared to meet the first candidate.

He reviewed the interview questions and, as he did so, he thought about how best to explain the challenges these young engineers might face. Without doubt, commissioning the plant would be a technical challenge. So far, it proved to be a greater challenge than even he anticipated when he joined DCL's management team. At first, he saw it as an attractive opportunity: heavy water production on a grand scale to meet the needs of Canada's CANDU nuclear power stations. It was Ontario's largest investment in electrical power generation since the taming of

Niagara Falls. However, there were some negatives, for example, the plant location already had a reputation for labor trouble and, partly because of Spevack's reputation, there were some troubling rumours about plant viability.

He knew something about Spevack's work on the Manhattan Project and the world's first Atomic Bomb. However, Spevack's credentials must have impressed the politicians. Otherwise why would they give him $50 million to test his ideas in a remote coal-mining town on the shores of Atlantic Canada?

Spevack was a kind of eminence grise around the plant. He appeared infrequently but had the biggest – and nearly always empty – office in the admin building. This made him a ghostly presence, spoken of in hushed terms. Since joining DCL, he had logged about 20 minutes in the great man's presence.

Ed knew Spevack's proposed process intimately. In past months, he watched the construction team assemble a jigsaw puzzle of pipes and equipment. He did a few back-of-the-envelope calculations and hoped Spevack's plant could produce heavy water.

Spevack's ongoing patent infringement feud with the United States Department of Energy discouraged contact with the DuPont engineers at the Savannah River plant. How he wished he could have had even a few days with senior process engineers at SRP: he had many questions that begged answers. He hadn't shared his innermost concerns with anyone and certainly not with the great man himself. Ed noticed that Spevack bristled with indignation at any suggestion that his design, and consequently the plant itself, was anything but perfect.

The location of the DCL plant posed special challenges in recruiting professional staff, especially engineers. He recognized this but had some difficulty in getting approval for hiring incentives such as generous moving allowances and above average salaries. When DCL's failure to hire a sufficient number of engineers threatened the commissioning schedule, the purse strings opened. He now felt confident that he could offer an attractive package to the two young engineers he was about to interview.

There was a knock on the door. He glanced at his meeting schedule, pushed back the chair, stepped from behind the desk and went to the door to meet Tim.

The meetings went well and at the conclusion of each interview he outlined what he felt was a very attractive compensation package, including a hefty fifty dollar a month premium over the usual starting rate of $650/mo.

He left Toronto and drove towards Queens University in Kingston, the next stop on his recruiting tour. As he drove down Highway 401, he thought about his interviews at U of T and felt that both Tim and Paul were promising hires. He certainly hoped so because plant construction was nearing completion and the commissioning schedule was tight.

When he returned to his office in Glace Bay, Ed issued job offers to Tim and Paul and was delighted when, two weeks later; he received letters of acceptance from each of them.

## GET A JOB

## A Tim Andreeff Story

*Sha na na na ... sha na na na na*
Get A Job - The Silhouettes - 1957, Written by The Silhouettes

In 1968, I was in my last year of engineering at the University of Toronto and job interviews were a new, and sometimes uncomfortable, experience. For example, one interviewer from a BC paper mill asked me (presumably using the stress theory of interviewing) if I was looking for a free trip to BC. "Uh no", I cleverly stammered and, as no surprise to me, I didn't get the job.

Early in my engineering studies, I met Paul and we became good friends. We went through four years together and over the years, we experienced our share of bars and parties together.

The Technical Manager from DCL, came to the U of T on a recruiting trip and we signed up for an interview. He interviewed us I and things went quite well. We received and accepted his job offers maybe in part because of the hefty fifty-dollar a month premium. I wondered whether he just wanted to get the best new engineers or if he couldn't get anyone else. In any event, He didn't say.

After exams Paul and I headed to Cape Cod in Paul's 1955 white Ford convertible with red leather upholstery. We planned to stay with Paul's girlfriend along the way. We made our way north through Maine, New Brunswick, and on to mainland Nova Scotia, aiming for the Eastern tip of Cape Breton and Glace Bay.

On the way up the TransCanada, west of Baddeck, Cape Breton, the Mounties stopped us. In 1968, getting stopped by the Mounties only meant one thing to a college student - narcs. I was so nervous when they asked me to get out of the car; I tripped and almost stumbled into the ditch. The Mountie grabbed my arm to steady me. Not a reassuring posture.

It soon became clear that the Mounties thought they had stopped a car with a trunk full of bootleg Ontario booze. As did the next pair of Mounties that stopped us. [To this day, Canada continues to deny free trade in alcohol across provincial borders.]

We arrived at the DCL plant and discovered that the entire Technical Section consisted of three lab techs, plus Paul and me! There was no office space for us, so we were installed in Spevack's office. No one knew where the great man usually hung out, but I never saw him in Glace Bay. Nonetheless, we were told to keep everything we took into the office on top of the desk so that if Spevack showed up unexpectedly, we could grab it all and exit fast.

A week after I arrived I had to fly back to Toronto for graduation, Paul opted to skip graduation and stayed behind. The following Saturday night, Paul and the three lab techs went cruising in Paul's 1955 white Ford convertible down Charlotte Street, the main 'drag' in Sydney. They got stopped by the cops and with open beer in the car they all ended up in the cooler. Thus, Ed's entire Technical Section was now out action: I was in Toronto, and everyone else was in jail.

# DENIS BOUVETTE

## WINNING THE LOTTERY

*A Denis Bouvette Story*

In 1976 I was appointed Director of Human Resources and Administration of the La Prade Heavy Water Plant in Bécancour, Québec. The day after my appointment I was told that I was part of a group of employees being "deported" to Glace Bay for a two-year training assignment on how to undertake a plant commissioning program for the La Prade plant.

We were approximately 12 people, mostly French Canadian, being invited to participate in this program. It's safe to say that several of the reassigned La Prade employees, most of whom spoke very little English, were dumbfounded. Consequently, each family had to make a very difficult decision. When I spoke with some of my La Prade friends afterward, it was clear that not everyone's sweetheart wanted to go. Some even broke into tears upon hearing the 'news'. These weren't tears of joy, either.

I went back home to advise my wife, Viviane, that we had won the lottery! Our first task was to locate Glace Bay on a map as we had no idea where we were going. My three children, Eric, aged 11, Valerie aged 9, and my youngest, Charles, aged 7, did not speak a word of English. Nonetheless, I accepted the reassignment, but few others did.

Most of the employees at the Glace Bay plant were born and raised in Cape Breton. The CFA's, [Come from Away], a term used by the locals to label anyone not born and raised in Cape Breton, experienced varying degrees of 'culture shock'.

I remember that our daughter, Valerie, sat in class from October to January without saying one word. Suddenly, in February, we caught her speaking pretty good English to a friend who had come home to play. We soon discovered that the teachers in Sydney schools were both patient and great psychologists. Today, our 3 adult children are fully bilingual and travel the world in pursuit of their work.

After a year of training, the La Prade employees were invited to a conference room and told by JC Paquin and Hugh VanAlstyne that the La

Prade Heavy Water Plant would be mothballed and most of us would be either be redeployed or terminated. Wow!

Although I did not know it at the time, the LaPrade plant was destined never to operate, not for a single day, the reason La Prade was closed is because, after it was built, the market for heavy water dried up.

My Glace Bay assignment turned out to be a one-way ticket. Nonetheless, I took on my assignment with enthusiasm and worked closely with Bob Brown, Head of Administration.

I assisted Bob with the hiring program for engineers and technicians for the plant. We had great difficulties in attracting professionals to come to Glace Bay with the usual newspaper ads. We decided to go to Calgary and Edmonton to canvass the market to give it a more personal touch. We collected the best pictures of the outdoors and a good description of the work at the plant and away we went.

Hugh had given us the authority to offer a $10,000 signing bonus if we found the right people. We spent a week in Alberta and were able to persuade 5 people to come to Glace Bay for follow-on interviews. I think, in the end we hired two! Such were the challenges in staffing the GBHWP.

# CARL TAYLOR

## WALKOUT

*Based on a Carl Taylor Story*

There always seemed to be something bothering the executive of Union Local 785. Perhaps it was simply a legacy of mining union activism. It was a particularly busy time for the HR/Labour Relations side of the business. Hugh VanAlstyne was Plant GM and Rollie was Operations Manager.

In a rare period of apparent calm, Carl went to Halifax with his family for a weekend break. They looked forward to the hotel pool, dining in Halifax restaurants and enjoying the sights and sounds of the Halifax waterfront. However, it was not to be.

When they arrived at the front desk of the hotel, there was a message that union Local 785 had just walked out. An illegal strike was underway, and Carl was needed back at the plant. Carl apologized to the hotel clerk, paid the cancellation fee, faced an obviously disappointed wife and hailed a cab to the airport. They waited at the airport for several hours and late on Friday evening they finally got seats on a flight back to Sydney.

Their flight arrived in Sydney after midnight. Carl made a phone call to Rollie who asked him to attend a meeting first thing in the morning. On Saturday morning Carl went into the plant and interviewed the supervisors and managers who had witnessed the walkout. He was told that there had been an impromptu union meeting and some union members were quite upset about work reassignments.

One of the maintenance foreman overheard the union conversation and he identified the person inciting Local 785 members to walk off the job. The 'inciter' was the first person to walk from the maintenance building to the security guard house to lead the walkout. Fortunately, the union understood some of the safety risks inherent in a walkout and essential services were maintained. However, the situation remained a very serious one.

Senior AECL Executives and the AECB were notified and, given the labor history of the original DCL plant, people in high places were decidedly nervous at the thought of an operating heavy water plant, full of poisonous H2S, without a full operating complement.

During subsequent discussions as to how management would respond, Carl got a confidential call from a member of the union. Carl agreed to protect his identity and subsequently called him 'Deep Throat', DT.

DT was very concerned about the actions the union might take if plant management responded to the walkout with heavy suspensions. Carl asked him to confirm the identity of the instigator. DT confirmed the name.

Thanks in part to the efforts of DT a meeting was arranged with the union executive to discuss the situation. The union executive insisted that the instigator attend the meeting and Carl agreed. The instigator had been a member of the executive for several years prior but was not at that time.

In subsequent discussions it became clear that the union knew how to talk itself 'out' but didn't know how to talk itself 'back in'. The union needed a face-saving gesture because many of their members were not happy at the prospect of no work, no pay and possible suspensions. Nonetheless, the blot of an illegal walkout couldn't simply be expunged with a conversation and a handshake. Something had to be done.

Rollie called a meeting of the senior management team to discuss the situation. Because it was a relatively early in the union-management relationship, he was concerned that the union local simply failed to understand the serious situation they had created, not just for them, but for the community and the future of the plant. He felt that the financial lifeline extended by the AECL Board was stretched to the breaking point and if this behaviour persisted, the plant would be doomed. Following consultation with Hugh, a formal complaint was filed with the Canada Labour Relations Board, [CLRB], asking that the walkout be declared illegal and that the union be held responsible for damages.

Carl then met with the instigator and told him that he faced a two-week suspension. The instigator got angry and, for a moment, Carl thought he might take a swing at him. When things cooled down a lengthy discussion resulted in a compromise. In return for an agreement that the instigator's suspension would stand but there would be no other suspensions, the union agreed to return to work. The instigator was suspended for two weeks for leading an illegal walkout. The union grieved the instigators suspension.

Several weeks later, an arbitrator convened a hearing. The arbitration questions were: Did the instigator lead the walkout? Was the suspension reasonable under the circumstances?

Company witnesses clearly established that the instigator had led the walkout. The arbitrator upheld the two-week suspension as reasonable under the circumstances.

Meanwhile, the national leadership of Energy and Chemical Workers considered placing the local union in trusteeship to mitigate their exposure to financial losses should the CLRB rule against them.

Subsequently, the [CLRB] ruled the walkout illegal and declared the Union liable for damages.

The regional representative of the OCAW, John Kane, knew that payment of damages would bankrupt the local. Kane met with Bob and Carl and pledged that the local union would never again stage an illegal walkout if AECL would not press their damage claim. To VanAlstyne's credit, he took the long view and dropped AECL's claim, thus sparing the union financial embarrassment and setting the stage for a more productive relationship.

During the remaining years of plant operation, the union never again staged an illegal walkout.

## BIG FOR EIGHT

### Based on a Carl Taylor Story

As Head of Administration and Personnel Manager for the GBHWP, Carl Taylor often wrestled with disability and compensation claims. A few employees played the 'comp game'. and worked while collecting compensation. It should be emphasized that most employees played by the rules.

Springtime in Cape Breton is little more than a feeble extension of winter. Some say that there are only two seasons in Cape Breton, 'winter' and 'tough sledding'.

One morning during the week before Christmas, Carl took a vacation day. He planned to spend the day with his parents who were visiting that week. Early in the morning he called his office and told Donna Somerville that he wouldn't be in that day but that he was available by phone if he was needed. Then, he went back to bed for a snooze before the day got underway. Shortly thereafter, Carl's wife, Georgina, 'Georgie', came upstairs to remind him that their new dishwasher, a Christmas gift, would be installed that morning and she hoped that the racket wouldn't disturb him.

The week prior, Carl had asked his next-door neighbor, a plumber, to do the dishwasher installation. His neighbour said that he needed to get an electrician to do that part of the installation, and at 8 AM that morning, the plumber and electrician arrived.

Georgie let the "contractors" in through the back door and they went downstairs to start the hookup. The electrician commented to Georgie on the fire extinguisher hanging by the back door with the AECL logo on it. Fire extinguishers were given to all employees as a safety performance reward. The electrician wanted to know if someone in the house worked for the plant. Georgie told him that her husband, Carl, worked at the Heavy Water Plant. The electrician looked surprised and then worried.

Meanwhile, Carl had dozed off and was awakened by the rattle and clank of the old dishwasher being rolled out and the new one being rolled in. There was much stomping about accompanied by the murmur of voices.

Shortly thereafter, Georgina came upstairs and as soon as she stepped through the door Carl knew something was amiss.

I think you should come downstairs," she said, with a nod towards the open door.

"Why?"

"There's someone here to put in the dishwasher and he says he shouldn't be here as he is on disability".

"What does he look like?"

"Big, round, red-faced, jolly looking."

"Did you hear his name?"

"I think the other guy called him 'Bump' or something like that."

Carl went down to see what was going on. An older man and a younger man were working. He did not recognize either of them. He went back upstairs and called Donna at the plant. He asked Donna to name electricians who were on disability. She named only one. Carl asked her to describe him. She did, and Carl guessed it was the electrician who was in his house that morning. The electrician should have been at home, recovering from his 'disability' or, if healthy enough, he should have been work instead of installing a dishwasher and collecting compensation benefits.

Carl then called the plant and talked to Donna and Derek Dymond. Derek had been suspicious of the electrician's 'disability' claim for some time.

Carl went downstairs and confronted the electrician who was by that time on the floor in the kitchen doing the final install.

The electrician looked at Carl and knew that something was up. The colour drained from his normally ruddy face.

"What are you doing here? Aren't you on workers compensation?" Carl asked.

"Just helping my buddy." Came the reply.

"Maybe so, but you're not supposed to be working here, or anywhere for that matter."

"Well, were almost done, give us about 15 minutes," the plumber said.

Carl replied, "You can't stay here, take your tools and leave."

Georgina pleaded, "What about my dishwasher?"

"The heavy lifting is done, I can finish up," said the boss.

Without a word, the electrician left the house and sat in the truck until the plumber finished the job. Then they left.

Carl then called Donna and brought her up to date.

A few days later, Carl met with a senior union official who asked him not to fire the violator, saying, "He's big for eight! He didn't know he was doing anything wrong. Don't punish him too severely."

Carl couldn't let it pass and couldn't agree to a slap on the wrist.

Another factor that played in the background was the rumoured plant closure and layoffs with compensation packages. Termination of employment would deny the offending employee his share of layoff compensation.

The employee was fired, and the union filed a grievance.

The case wound its way through the usual stages until arbitration. John Kane argued 'entrapment', that management had somehow set the employee up. The arbitrator dismissed that argument as patently false.

However, the arbitrator ruled in the union's favour using 'creative logic' citing a provision in the disability program allowed for 'work rehabilitation'. The electrician/employee was reinstated with loss of pay but no loss of seniority. The union was very happy with the 'win'. Carl decided not to appeal. It was a sobering lesson for all and it underscored the serious consequences of abuse of disability insurance and Workers Compensation.

Subsequently, the employee enjoyed the full benefit of plant closure compensation.

# GERRY ARMITAGE

## WEST YORKSHIRE LAD

*Based on a Gerry Armitage Story*

Gerry was born in 1944 in a small coal-mining village in West Yorkshire, United Kingdom. He came from a coal mining family who worked in the coal mines of West Yorkshire. Although not undersea, West Yorkshire coal mines resembled those of Cape Breton in work methods, organization and culture[77].

He was one of four children, each of who were well educated and became accomplished farmers, coal miners, and midwives. His family suffered a coal mining tragedy when two of his father's uncles were killed in a West Yorkshire coal mine. His father subsequently left the coal mines and became a successful business owner. Gerry's mother came from a wealthy family who owned a textile-manufacturing mill.

The story of Gerry and his wife, Christine[78] began in the 1950s when they met as students in classes at Ossett Grammar School. Gerry graduated in 1966 from the University of Bradford with a major in chemistry. Christine graduated from Sheffield University and began her teaching career in 1967. Christine's father and his family were coal miners. Christine also understood Cape Breton's coal mining culture.

For a time, Gerry worked in the steel industry, thus unwittingly creating a future Cape Breton connection. Much like the Cape Bretoner's of his generation, including the author, Gerry realized that steel making was a 'losing' industry. Old-line methods of production were obsolete and

---

[77] Following its 'discovery', Cape Breton became an important French outpost. In the 18th century it figured prominently in the struggles between England, France and the American colonies. Nova Scotia's history contains many stories of coal-mining disasters, such as, the Springhill disasters of 1956 and 1958, the 1979 Glace Bay Disaster at #26 Colliery, and the Westray disaster of 1992. There were countless other coal-mining accidents and many deaths going all the way back to the founding of Louisbourg in 1713.

[78] Gerry and Christine have two adult, children, Heather and James.

the relationship between management and workers was fractious. Strikes were endemic...in Yorkshire as well as in Cape Breton.


## ONTARIO HYDRO

In early 1968, with bleak prospects for a future in a modern industrial setting, Gerry began a serious job search. Coincidentally, Ontario Hydro was recruiting people in the UK for jobs at the Pickering Nuclear Power Station. Gerry applied and was interviewed and, as he subsequently said, was absolutely astounded at the difference in approach between Ontario Hydro and the UK Nuclear Power Agency.

Shortly thereafter, Gerry received a job offer from Ontario Hydro to work as a health physicist, with the promise of an assignment to Pickering. Gerry and Christine talked it over and made a life-altering decision to emigrate to Canada. On June 30, 1968, Gerry left for Canada with Christine's promise that she would join him eight weeks later.

Gerry arrived in Canada at Ontario's Toronto airport on Friday, July 1, Canada-Day. He stepped off the plane wearing a thick wool suit and a heavy trench coat. He wilted under the 30C temperature and 95% relative humidity. Rumours of polar bears, glaciers, and mounds of snow were quickly discounted. Gerry hailed a taxi and checked into his Toronto hotel room.

On Monday, July 4, he went to Ontario Hydro's Head office at 620 University Avenue where he met Dr. Tom Hamilton and Al Frey. Dr. Hamilton was the Assistant Director of Medical Services for Ontario Hydro. During a pleasant meeting, Gerry was told that his initial assignment would be in the Health Physics Department, working for Gary Vivian, at Douglas Point Generating Station. Douglas Point was Ontario Hydro's prototype nuclear power station, in Bruce County[79] on Lake Huron. Gerry was issued an Ontario Hydro briefcase and Al Frey arranged

---

[79] Until the advent of nuclear power plants, Bruce County, 200 miles northwest of Toronto, was farming country. As it turned out, Bruce County produced well educated young people who proved well suited to the rigours of nuclear power operations.

to take Gerry to the town of Kincardine. Kincardine and Port Elgin were the principal residential towns for Ontario Hydro Employees.

Gerry and Al left for Kincardine and as it happened, there was a brewery strike in Ontario in the summer of 1968. Frey made a side trip to Formosa, Ontario, where he purchased four cases of beer at a non-union brewery.

They arrived at the Bruce Inn, in Kincardine, where Gerry was to stay for the next two months at Ontario Hydro's expense. Ontario Hydro also offered 'free' bus transportation from Kincardine to the Douglas Point station, 20 miles away.

The next day, Gerry got up early, and dressed for work. He wore his best suit, a white shirt and a tie and left the inn. He walked several blocks to the Bank of Montréal where he waited for the promised bus transportation to Douglas Point.

He was the first one to arrive at the designated bus stop and, as time ticked on, he wondered, "Am I in the only one here? Did I miss the bus?" A few minutes later, Gerry watched a man in his late 30s approach the bus stop. He carried an Ontario Hydro briefcase, just like Gerry's. The man wore a loose-fitting pair of slacks, a short sleeve open neck shirt and carried a newspaper, the Globe and Mail, tucked under his arm. Gerry stepped forward, extended his hand and said, "I'm Gerry Armitage, I've just arrived from the UK, I'm starting in health physics at Douglas point, I'm working for Gary Vivian."

The man said, "Hi Gerry, my name is Sam Horton."

Gerry inquired, " Sam, what do you do at Douglas Point?"

Sam replied, "I'm the Station Manager."

Several other people arrived at the bus stop and Sam Horton introduced Gerry to each of them. Gerry was impressed…he got to meet the big boss on his first day…it was a good beginning.

Gerry began his work at Douglas Point and soon learned that the station was in a difficult operational situation. Several major issues had to be overcome if the station was to operate successfully. For example, there was heavy water leakage from valve stems and the heat transport pumps, there was a buildup of Cobalt-60 giving rise to high radiation fields, and there were problems with the on-power fuelling machines[80] Douglas point was the 'prototype' CANDU[81] power station and it was vital to fix these problems and apply these 'fixes' to the Pickering[82] station if CANDU was to have any hope of commercialization.

For a young man born in Yorkshire England, Ontario Hydro offered Gerry an opportunity to participate in the pioneering stages of nuclear power development in Canada. There were challenges aplenty…not the least of which was getting a reliable supply of heavy water.

Thanks to strong leadership of Canada's nuclear pioneers at AECL and Ontario Hydro, and the talent and teamwork of people like Gerry, the Douglas Point problems were resolved, and, in the fall of 1968, Douglas Point GS was declared "in service". Canada's first 'commercial' nuclear power station produced electricity for Ontario consumers.

This was 'a big deal' and Gerry was present when Pierre Trudeau, [father of Canada's current Prime Minister, Justin Trudeau], declared the

---

[80] On-power refuelling was big selling point for CANDU reactors, a significant advantage in operating efficiency compared with the other reactors of the day. If it worked!

[81] Uranium fuel offers an energy content well beyond coal. A cubic inch of CANDU uranium fuel contains as much energy as a ton of coal. Two-thousand MW can be pictured as two-hundred thousand, one-hundred-watt light bulbs, blazing 24x7x365...a constantly burning square mile of light...you could see it from the moon...a lotta energy!

[82] Pickering was Ontario's billion-dollar electrical power bet. Pickering, a 2000 Megawatt, [MW], CANDU power station, hugged the shores of Lake Ontario, east of Toronto. Pickering, at 2000 MW, was ten times bigger than Douglas Point and a billion-dollar financial commitment. Nobody talked billions in the 1960s. C.D. Howe, a Federal Cabinet Minister and 'Minister of Everything' in Canada during WW2 was roundly criticized for exclaiming, "What's a million?" when asked about a million-dollar loss in a government project. Thus, Canada, the Province of Ontario, AECL and Ontario Hydro had each placed long term, multi-billion-dollar bets on the future of CANDU nuclear power. The 20th century political, financial, and reputational stakes were about as high as Canada's bet on the Canadian Pacific Railway in the 19th century.

official operation of Douglas Point GS to be 'a significant milestone' for Canada's nuclear power industry.

As a Gerry said later, " It was an amazing experience to witness and participate in this team, the ups and down, the victories and disappointments."

Gerry joined the heavy water production business in early 1970, when he volunteered to join the Bruce Heavy Water Plant team.

## PORT HAWKESBURY

In May of 1970, Gerry was assigned to the Port Hawkesbury Heavy Water Plant for training and familiarization at the operating plant. It was a wonderful learning opportunity since he had access to the Lummus process engineering team, plant designers, and people from every type of chemical process facility in Canada as well as chemical engineers from the Savannah River plant in South Carolina.

Accommodation was tight in Port Hawkesbury and Gerry and his family had to find an apartment in Antigonish, 38 miles away. Other families living there included BHWP staff, Jim Dalton, Paul Core, Dave Purvis and George Grichtmeier.

Antigonish was a relatively cultivated town because of St. Francis Xavier University, SFX. There was a large hospital, good restaurants and many retail stores. The 38-mile drive was no fun following the end of a long night shift.

Gerry enrolled as a part time student at SFX and took a course in Medieval Theology. He also joined the SFX rugby team and was selected to play for the Province of Nova Scotia. Christine became student at SFX in September and she completed her B.Ed. degree in June of 1971.

Gerry went to Bruce in January 1971 for one week, then he went back to Port Hawkesbury until July 1971. During this time, he was AECL's liaison, providing feedback to the project team for the new BHWP plant. It was during this period that AECL was directed to resurrect Deuterium of Canada's failed Glace Bay Heavy Water Plant. The plant had been idle since 1969 when DCL went broke.

## BHWP

Gerry returned to BHWP in July 1971 and was assigned to write commissioning procedures. However, he wanted to be a Shift Supervisor and he discussed it with the Production Manager, Bill Hatton. Hatton was non-committal. A few days later Gerry was called into the Plant Manager's office. Bob Icely asked him to complete the Safety Manual and to raise Purchase Orders for equipment for the safety program.

Shortly thereafter Gerry was appointed Plant Safety Engineer and was transferred into the Production Department. A new Shift Foreman was assigned to assist Gerry.

A week later Bill Hatton told him that the Shift Supervisors had recommended that Gerry's assistant be fired for non-performance and asked Gerry to deliver the bad news. Gerry successfully argued that he had no reason to fire the man. Hatton gave him 3 months to turn the man around. Gerry succeeded in doing this and the man became the plant's resource in fire fighting and did all the work setting it up.

This Safety job was completed by mid December 1971 and then Gerry was appointed Shift Supervisor for C shift. He attended a one-week supervisory training program at the Ontario Hydro Training Centre and begin shift work after Christmas. Tim Andreeff, recently arrived from the failed DCL plant in Glace Bay, was the shift engineer on C shift.

Gerry remained on shift at BHWP for three years, until late 1974. By that time, he was ready for something new and he talked to Bill Hatton about what came next. He wanted to join the project team preparing to commission the new plant, BHWP B. However, it did not happen.

## LAPRADE

Gerry joined AECL in early January 1975 as Production Superintendent for the La Prade Heavy Water Plant which was under construction. J.C.Paquin was LaPrade's General Manager and Hugh VanAlstyne was the Production Manager and Ken Round was Technical Manager. Subsequently, Hugh and Ken were assigned to BHWP on training assignments.

From January to early May 1975, Gerry worked on projects for LaPrade until there was a 'pause' in the project.

Mike Joyce also had joined the La Prade project was being pushed to come to Glace Bay HWP. He and Anne came to visit Gerry and Christine and Gary tried to persuade him to come to Glace Bay but instead went to work for the Federal government.

## ASSIGNMENT

In May, J.C Paquin invited Gerry to accompany him to Glace Bay on an assignment. There was growing concern in AECL that things were not going well at Glace Bay. Rehabilitation was about 75% complete and utilities commissioning was underway. Their subsequent report validated AECL's concerns.

The management line up at Glace Bay at that time was:

John Sproule, General Manager, a long-time AECL employee. John's last job was Reactor Superintendent at either NRX or NRU in Chalk River.

Kjeld Jensen, Technical Manager. Kjeld came from Polysar in Sarnia, ON.

Arthur Pratt, Maintenance Manager. Art came from ARAMCO in Saudi Arabia, an oil processing plant.

Bob Keating, Commissioning Manager. Gerry knew Bob when Bob was AECL's Assistant Project Manager at the BHWP in 1970/71

Gerry Harley, Production Superintendent. Armitage knew Harley from Port Hawkesbury where Armitage was Harley's Shift Engineer.

Bob Brown. Personnel Manager, Bob had just taken over this function.

Gerry Coleman, Supply and Stores Manager. Gerry was a long-term presence at Glace Bay.

Fred Hill, Plant Chemist. Gerry knew Fred from Port Hawkesbury where they sometimes played bridge as a team. They were once asked to leave the Antigonish Bridge Club because they were too boisterous for some of the staid older members.

Barbara MacDonald and Audrey Gouthro were plant secretaries and Bev MacIntosh was the Plant Nurse.

Following their assignment, Gerry and J.C. were supposed to return to Glace Bay to help improve the situation. Gerry went back after the July 1st holiday of 1975, but J.C. did not go.

## GLACE BAY RETURN

Soon afterward, Gerry was told that he had no job at LaPrade. He either accepted a job at Glace Bay otherwise he had no job. Upon arrival he was appointed Acting Production Manager.

In his new role, Gerry visited the Seaboard Power Plant, which was owned and operated by Nova Scotia Power. Seaboard delivered process steam to the Glace Bay plant. It was Gerry's first ever visit to a coal fired power plant. He entered the turbine hall through a hole in a brick wall, not a confidence-builder! He walked around the plant with a supervisor and thought how unlikely it was to rely on this decrepit plant.

Subsequently, Gerry was a key player in plant commissioning and early operations. He tried to persuade Bob Keating to stay on as commissioning activity wound down, but Keating was committed to leave.

Gerry left Glace Bay in 1979, guessing correctly, as it turned out, that Glace Bay would be shut down because of the growing heavy water supply imbalance stemming from poor CANDU reactor sales. Glace Bay was the high cost producer and at that time Bruce was producing hundreds of tons of heavy water each year. Gerry felt it was time to move on after four hard years at Glace Bay.

## IAEA, CHERNOBYL, ROMANIA

Gerry returned to the Bruce site of Ontario Hydro in October 1979 and got back into the radiation safety until 1982 when he moved to Pickering GS, near Toronto, as Manager of Health Physics Services.

In 1984 he worked on a new approach to Radiation Safety for the International Atomic Energy Authority, IAEA. In 1986 he went to the USSR with a group from Ontario Hydro to help with the cleanup after the Chernobyl accident. In 1988 he also audited a US power plant in King of Prussia, Pennsylvania, and in 1989 he joined a team to audit the Smolensk NPP in the USSR.

On 2 November 1992 he joined AECL's Start Up Assistance team for the Cernavoda NPP in Romania. The move made economic and professional sense but it seriously disrupted Christine's teaching career. Their daughter, Heather, was studying engineering at Queens and their son James completed Grade 13 in 1993 and he then went to the University of Toronto, U of T. Heather and James came to Romania for Christmas of 1993.

Gerry's job in Romania was to set up the Radiation Safety Program. Originally the Romanians were to supply heavy water for the Cernavoda Plant from their Drobeta Heavy Water Plant near Turnu-Severin. The plant was late and failed to provide sufficient heavy water. AECL agreed to lend/lease heavy water from Canada. The problem was that no one in AECL new whether the heavy water would ever be returned.

Keith Bradley and Gerry were asked to undertake a review of the Drobeta Heavy Water Plant to determine its capability. They were given two days, 7-8 May of 1994, to assess the plant and its power and steam supply. They issued a report on 25 May 1994. Their report highlighted both safety and operational issues but supported the lend/lease arrangement with AECL.

Their report estimated a 20% probability of an employee fatality in the next three years of operation. This prediction created an uproar in the Bucharest news media. Gerry and Keith were labelled 'economic saboteurs'. Christine received the news with deep concern and, not surprisingly, she wanted to catch the next plane home![83]

---

[83] ROMANIA - Social and economic malaise had been present in socialist Romania for quite some time, especially during the austerity years of the 1980s. Riots, street violence and murder in several Romanian cities over the course of roughly a week in 1989 led the Romanian strongman Ceausescu to flee the capital city on 22 December with his wife, Elena, who was also Deputy Prime Minister. Evading capture by hastily departing via helicopter effectively portrayed the couple as both fugitives and acutely guilty of accused crimes. They were captured and tried by drumhead military tribunal. They were convicted on all charges, sentenced to death, and immediately executed on Christmas Day 1989, becoming the last persons condemned to death and executed in Romania.

During the evening of 23 June 1994, a power failure occurred at the plant and H2S was released into the effluent during a power outage. The effluent ran in an open ditch and under a public highway. Four employees died, and several others were rendered unconscious.

## PRODUCTION MANAGER

*In Gerry's own words.*

In late September 1975 I was still Acting Production Manager. I was on my way back to Sydney and I bought a copy of the Globe and Mail at the airport. In the Report on Business section I saw an advertisement for 'Production Manager , Glace Bay Heavy Water Plant'. I remember telling Christine when I arrived home that AECL were advertising "my job" and nobody had told me about it. I decided not to mention it at work and I did not apply for the job.

Weeks later John Sproule asked me if I would help him to interview some candidates. Feigning innocence, I asked what job they were being interviewed for. After some spluttering he told me it was for "my job" Production Manager. I agreed to help him. We interviewed two or 3 candidates, but none were suitable.

Afterwards, he asked me if I would apply for the job and I said no I would not. Since I was already doing the job I saw no reason to apply for it.

On 1 Nov 1975 John called me to his office and handed me a letter offering me the job of Production Manager. The letter said, "as the result of an internal competition". I accepted.

Acknowledging Gerry Harley's important contribution, Gerry Armitage said, *"He was essentially holding the Production Dept. together when I got there. It would have been really difficult to make progress without him in the early days. Gerry Harley did persuade Al Niemi to stay, which was a big plus."*

## PREMIER GERALD REGAN

*In Gerry's own words.*

When I began working at Glace Bay, I lived in the Holiday Inn for a few weeks, until AECL moved me into the 18th Floor apartment at Cabot House on Kings Road. My routine involved a weekend return to Ottawa every third week and this went on until February 1976. On flights from Ottawa to Halifax on a couple of occasions I sat with Gerald Regan on the flights, he was always interested in progress at Glace Bay.

## LABOUR RELATIONS

*In Gerry's own words.*

My introduction to labour relations at Glace bay began in late July 1975 when contract negotiations began. The labour relations manger from Ottawa chaired the talks. I joined Bob Brown, Turk Stewart and Art Pratt as plant representatives. I was appalled by the confrontational stance of the labour relations people. At lunch on the first day our negotiation team met to discuss operator training, classification levels and pay scales. The AECL Head Office proposed a scheme used at AECL's Chalk River Research Facilities. This scheme involved fixed positions and levels for each different operation in the plant. This was contrary to the concept I was used to, where every operator was trained to work in any position and on any equipment and the only specialist positions were Control Panel Operators. Operators would be trained and promoted as required.

I explained that since I was relatively new to the plant I had not finished formulating our staffing and training plan, but I wanted something like the Ontario Hydro model. I felt that the best operational models for plants involves flexibility in work assignments. This idea caused great consternation from our human resources people and at the lunch break the gentleman from Ottawa began chewing me out for not following the party line and he abused the Ontario Hydro model. At which point I suggested he could apologise for the abuse or else he could leave for Ottawa and let plant people handle negotiations. Two days later he left the negotiations and Bob Brown ran them from that point onward.

# BOB SISSINGH

## TOFFLER AND HEAVY WATER

*A BOB SISSINGH STORY*

*Author's Introduction: Bob Sissingh has a unique sense of humour and. it was on display from the very first moment he joined the Bruce Heavy Water Plant. When he reviewed the first draft of this book he suggested a new title: 'Heavy Water Production in Canada Is the Era Where Careers Were Built, Billions of Dollars Were Wasted, And At Least One Village Was Destroyed'.*

It would not surprise me that the futurist, Alvin Toffler[84], played a role in the decision to build heavy water plants across the country. He was influential and firm in the prediction of world wide shortage of energy, oil and other fuels. He expressed this in his book "Future Shock", published in 1970. His predictions turned out to be wrong, wrong and wrong again. Years later oil and gas supply were abundant. Everybody had second thoughts. Global warming was not even on, under or above the radar. Over the next few years heavy water plants were decommissioned and even today, in 2018, they are still demolishing parts of the Bruce plant.

The "Chernobyl" disaster in 1986 didn't help. Suddenly, the prospects of building more nuclear plants were bleak and there was a surplus of heavy water. This is all hindsight wisdom. Ontario residents are still paying off the old Ontario Hydro billions of debts.

The heavy water plant in Port Hawkesbury hired personnel from all over Canada but not many from Port Hawkesbury. Then the Gulf oil refinery was built on the same site and, three years later, it was decommissioned and removed.

Dr. Jerome S. Spevack was the co-developer of the "dual temperature exchange sulphide process. His partner was Dr. Victor Thayer. They were partners at the time and worked as a team. Dr. Thayer's name is rarely mentioned because Spevack's wife was a shrewd and powerful lawyer in

---

[84] Alvin Toffler (October 4, 1928 – June 27, 2016) was an American writer, futurist and a businessman known for his works discussing modern technologies, including the digital revolution, and the communication revolution, with emphasis on their effects on cultures worldwide.

the US and she immediately patented the production of heavy water process under Spevack's name. General Electric paid Spevack 1.5 million dollars, to use the process in Port Hawkesbury. I don't know how much Ontario Hydro had to pay.

DCL used Burns and Roe as design engineers for their plant. I had about 6 Burns and Roe engineers working for me at Princeton Plasma Physics Laboratory (PPPL) where I was Branch Head. They were good system engineers, but I never saw any strength in their process engineering department.

I visited GBHWP once, maybe twice. I was asked by the Horton brothers, [Sam, Elgin][85], to investigate the need for the ring of fire, [Gas Dispersion System, GDS], around the towers. Johnny Cash sang about it! I did not recommend it, [they did it anyway].

When I was there, GBHWP gave a party for all their personnel. I was invited too. When I entered the room, the women were sitting on one side of the tables and the men on the other side. Obviously, I seated myself on the women's side. They heard my Dutch accent, so they asked where I came from and I said I was born and raised in the Maritimes. This was not a lie since Holland is a maritime country! The next question was where in the Maritimes and I said Flushing. This was not a lie. The English changed the city's name Vlissingen to Flushing. The women looked puzzled, but I got no further questions. When the servers came each table got a bottle of wine which I put under the table. The second server put another bottle of wine on the table. I thought it was quite clever of me. It did not take long before other men took part in the conversations and one man, maybe a husband, joined the group.

---

[85] Sam and Elgin Horton were key players in the development of Nuclear Power for Ontario Hydro. Sam passed away in 2013 at the age of 80.

# ROLLIE MACINNIS

## BOOT ALLOWANCE

*A Rollie MacInnis Story*

The collective agreement with Local 785 provided each member of the all male local with a payment to enable purchase of a new pair of work boots each year.

Frank tenTusscher, our Accountant, said that it cost an average of $20 to issue a separate cheque for the 'boot allowance' and he recommended we reimburse it via payroll deduction.

During contract negotiations I put this proposal to the local union and, surprisingly, I received a very strenuous 'push back'. I was confused by this reaction because, after all, money is money no matter how you get it.

Hugh VanAlstyne understood what was behind the resistance and he explained that a separate cheque could be hidden from the spouse/wife/girlfriend and used as beer money or for some other purpose better suited to men. He further explained that the average pair of work boots lasted two to 3 years and that the 'boot allowance' cheque was really a small perk for union men which, in the interest of good labour relations, we should agree with.

When management returned to the negotiating table, it was agreed that a separate check would be issued for the 'boot allowance'. Lesson learned.

## IT'S A DRILL

*A Rollie MacInnis Story*

Early one morning, I met with Hugh in his office to go over current operations. Our meeting was interrupted by a call from Hugh's boss, Head of AECL Heavy Water Projects. I sat and listened to Hugh carry his end of the conversation. The conversation sounded routine. How is the plant operating these days? What's the forecast for heavy water production this month? The conversation was interrupted when the plant control room announced the routine test of emergency signals over the public-address system. The announcement went something like,

"ATTENTION, ATTENTION, this is a test of the emergency system."

The announcement was followed by three signals, ALERT, EMERGENCY, and ALL CLEAR.

Each signal had a distinctive sound a short STACCATO BEEP, a WARBLE, a CONTINUOUS TONE, after which, the control room signed off and the speaker in Hugh's office went silent.

While I couldn't hear the other side of the conversation, I heard Hugh say,

"It's a Drill."

There was a brief pause and then Hugh said,

"It's a test, boss."

I assumed that his boss was worried about what was going on.

Hugh repeated, more loudly this time,

"It's just a test!"

Hugh looked at me, rolled his eyes, and repeated,

"It's just a test, we do it every morning!"

After several rounds of this gainsaying conversation, Hugh lost his patience and shouted, "IT'S JUST A F...ING TEST!"

Things settled down and the conversation resumed a more amiable tone and concluded shortly thereafter.


## LEAD APRONS

Unionized clerical workers, all female, had their own union local but took a less militant stance on issues than their trades and operating brothers.

For some reason, the introduction of a high output photo copier became a health and safety issue. Clerical union representatives worried that radiation from the copiers might be harmful. Notwithstanding that AECL represented Canada's expertise in all forms of radiation, the union could not be persuaded to alter their demand for protection.

Therefore, lead aprons were purchased such that employees could choose to wear them when making copies. We decided that safety rules would not mandate their use, it was to be an employee choice.

Not surprisingly, within weeks of the introduction of lead aprons, they were worn less often. They were heavy, hot, and uncomfortable.

It's not always a bad idea to grant some employee demands, especially if the cost is modest and you can make progress on other issues.

A clear case where the expression, "Get the lead out!" truly meant something.


## ANGRY BIRD

When job vacancies occurred, it was common practice to post a vacancy notice on bulletin boards and ask for applications from interested employees. On one occasion, a Maintenance Clerk position in the Maintenance Department became vacant and the job was 'posted'.

It is safe to assume that every workplace has its characters and the Glace Bay plant was no different. In this case, the person interested in the position was a confident, often outspoken, woman. She could, and did, hold her own in any conversations with anyone.

She, [name withheld], was smart and outspoken and she marched into the supervisor's office with a piece of paper in her hand. She was 'wound up' about something. The Supervisor asked her to take a seat, but she refused and slammed the paper on his desk. "Read this," she said.

As soon as he saw it he knew it was a job posting for the Maintenance Clerk position. He looked up and shrugged a 'so what?' She leaned over his desk until their noses were practically touching. Then she lowered her voice and said, "Who do I have to [expletive deleted] to get this job!" She meant it sarcastically.

The supervisor was not usually lost for words, but he was that time. The best he could do what to tell her that she had to make an application just like everyone else. He could tell by the look of disgust on her face that she thought that even if she did make an application she wouldn't get the job. There wasn't much more he could say but he told her that she would get a 'fair shake'. She turned to leave, and he picked up the paper and asked her if she wanted it. She looked over her shoulder, laughed and said, "You keep it and...," her voice trailed off and she walked out the door. He guessed where she wanted him to file it.

## CHEMICAL COMPANY

### A Rollie MacInnis Story

In the early 1980s, under the leadership of Jim Donnelly[86] there was some restructuring of AECL. Heavy Water Projects transitioned into the Chemical Company and J.H. [Howard] Langstaff, a new Vice President, appeared.

I don't remember much about Howard Langstaff except meeting him in Hugh's office. He said that the heavy water business had an uncertain future and we might survive for a few more years.

I came away from the meeting feeling confused about Langstaff's plans for the Chemical Company. We had worked and fought hard for our place in the Canadian nuclear industry and I wasn't prepared to concede anything regarding our capability. I was probably blind to the 'handwriting'.

In 1981 Langstaff was appointed Vice-President, Corporate Planning and Bill Hatton was appointed Executive Vice-President of the Chemical Company. Roger Jeffreys succeeded Bill at Port Hawkesbury and, Hugh

---

[86] In 1978, Jim Donnelly left his job as CEO of Stadler Hurter, to accept the position of President and CEO of AECL. Jim retired in 1989 after 11 years of service. He oversaw the closure of the Cape Breton plants. Following Donnelly's departure, Stan Hatcher became Acting President and CEO and was confirmed in the position later. Hatcher had a close connection to the heavy water plants and served as AECL Liaison at the Bruce Heavy Water Plant. When the AECL President's job opened, Don Lawson, VP at Sheridan Park, was an obvious candidate for the position. I found out, much later on, in 2017, from Don's Secretary, Cecile Kennedy, that Don was very disappointed at not being chosen. Don's Sheridan Park colleagues shared in his disappointment. Coincidentally, on 14 December 2007, Prime Minister Stephen Harper announced the appointment of Hugh MacDiarmid as Chief Executive Officer (CEO) of AECL. MacDiarmid was President and CEO of Lumonics Inc. He was my boss when I worked there as VP, General Manager of Lumonics, Kanata.

was made responsible for both plants. I was appointed General Manager of the Glace Bay Plant.

The Chemical Company had several divisions such as, Human Resources, led by Doug Jordan, and Finance led by, Harold Morrison. Harold's family came from Northern Cape Breton and during visits to the plants, Harold found the time to take the Englishtown ferry to that part of the island.

Bill Hatton was a colleague and friend from our days at the Bruce Heavy Water Plant. I have very fond memories of Bill, his wife Ruth and his family when we lived in Port Elgin. We spent many pleasant afternoons, with our families, on the sandy beaches of Lake Huron.

Bill had a lot of experience in the chemical industry, not all of which was entirely pleasant. I was told by JC Paquin that Bill was once the manager of a plant in Montréal East that suffered a fatality resulting from a serious incident. That explained Bill's safety obsession.

Not long after Bill's Chemical Company appointment, I met him in his office in Tunney's Pasture, Ottawa. Bill's inner sanctum had ankle-deep broadloom carpet, rich mahogany furniture, floor length draperies, coffee table lamps, and brass doorknobs.

Bill's engineering team was led by Ian Smith, assisted by Bob Keating. Keating had a long history in heavy water construction going all the way back to the construction of the Bruce Heavy Water Plant and the rehabilitation of the original Glace Bay plant. Smith had a habit of using the French expression *d'accord* as often as possible, albeit with a Scots accent.

Hatton insisted that Ian Smith's team review and approve the engineering projects that the operating heavy water plants proposed. Ian's team were contract administrators not plant engineering experts and they assigned their reviews to outside contractors.


## MEETING JAKE

*A Rollie MacInnis Story*

In 1984 the miners union, District 26, UMW, went on strike. Strikers picketed the roads leading to the plant's steam supplier, NSP's Seaboard Plant, blocking coal deliveries.

Stan McPhee, the Seaboard Manager suggested I should meet with the President of the UMW local union, Jake Campbell, and negotiate passage through their picket lines.

By all accounts, Jake Campbell was a Cape Breton character of the first magnitude. He was short, balding and disheveled in appearance. It was not easy to tell if he had teeth. He was deceptively intelligent and politically savvy. One didn't get to be President of the UMW otherwise.

Cape Breton humour often depicts the little man bringing the big man down. That type of humour played particularly well with UMW membership. Jake Campbell was a master story teller in that vein.

I took Stan's advice and asked Jerry Coleman[87] to arrange a meeting with Jake Campbell. A few days later Jerry peered around the open door of my office to say, "Jake Campbell is here."

I went to Jerry's office and was introduced to Jake Campbell. Following the introductions, I attempted to break the ice by saying, "I understand that you and Jerry go way back."

Jake said with an apparently toothless grin, *"I knew Jerry when he was running around Glace Bay with his dick in his hand!"*

I was rendered speechless...a feat in itself!

It seemed like minutes, but probably seconds, before I recovered from this unexpected combination of humour and embarrassment. Jerry looked on, unperturbed...he'd seen it before.

I subsequently learned that experienced negotiators will deliver statements deliberately calculated to put an adversary off stride. If so, it worked in this instance.

I remember Jake Campbell's sly, grinning, face, assessing my reaction with apparent satisfaction. I knew then and there that there was no way we were going to get any concessions from the UMW.

---

[87] Jerry Coleman was a long-time resident of Glace Bay. He worked at the plant since the DCL days in the 1960s. He had a practical view of the world of purchasing. About the corrupting influences of product and service vendors, Jerry quoted an old time, somewhat shady, purchasing agent whose advice was, "If you can't eat it or drink it, don't take it!" Jerry was a man of integrity and was well-liked. He ran an excellent Purchasing and Stores operation.

However, I had a trick up my sleeve and, with Stan's cooperation, we constructed a road through property owned by AECL and bypassed the UMW picket lines. We enabled coal supply to Stan thanks to the cooperation of DEVCO, the local mining company.

## NEGOTIATING

*A Rollie MacInnis Story*

One of my early shortcomings as a leader/manager was my lack of good communication skills. Particularly in my early years, I was far more interested in what I was thinking and saying and much less interested in what others were hearing and understanding. This deficiency became much more apparent during union negotiations.

During my first performance review with Hugh, he gave me the task of negotiating a new collective agreement with ASEA, the independent technical/supervisory employees union. Hugh followed these negotiations closely and insisted on a post meeting review with me. He'd ask questions like, "What issues were discussed? What did you say? What did they say?" His instructions and advice were invaluable. Gradually, I learned to listen and pay attention to what was being said and to read faces, body language, and to respond on that basis. I worked on my communication skills.

Later, I led the negotiating team for a renewed collective agreement with ECW local 785. This was an even bigger challenge because I squared off with John Kane, a very experienced negotiator for ECW. John knew the negotiation ropes, better than I did but I had Bob Brown with me and Bob's experience was a life saver.

I encountered a major problem near the end of my first set of negotiations when I presented our money offer. Money is at the top of the union list of demands but is the last thing to be resolved, as it was in this case.

In the days prior to the negotiation session, I had discussed the money offer with Hugh. Hugh was very thoughtful about this and he instructed me to present our 'final' offer at the next negotiation session. He made it clear that if the offer was not accepted, there might be what he called a 'gumdrop', a few more cents per hour as a 'kicker' to seal the deal. However, he said that he could not guarantee any more money and besides the union had to believe that they got everything that management had on the table otherwise they would feel 'snookered' and resentful thereafter. Thus, I had to make a 'final' offer work as best I could.

Near the end of the negotiating session the atmosphere was expectant, and I put our 'final' offer to John Kane. It was a generous offer that should have met the union's every demand. As usual, John said he would discuss our offer with 'the membership' and get back to me.

A day later, I got a call from John saying that the offer was rejected. I was surprised and so was John. John called me again to say that we needed to have another session and that I would have to explain our offer more clearly since the union executive misunderstood my 'complex' offer.

I discussed the situation with Hugh and he came up with a small 'gumdrop', another nickel.

We had another session and with Bob's advice to 'keep it simple' I explained it again and offered the extra gumdrop, a face saver for the union, and for me.

The offer was accepted, and negotiations concluded on a high note.

In the years that followed, I prepared for union negotiation weeks in advance and carefully studied the contract, the union demands, our responses and arguments. I learned to enjoy the challenges of communication effectively[88] .


## WHITNEY PIER FRIEND

*A Rollie MacInnis Story*

One of our employees at the Glace Bay plant was a childhood acquaintance of mine from Whitney Pier. I got to know him during visits to my grandmother's house at 5 East St. His father was a prominent member of Trinity United Church who signed my Cradle Roll

---

[88] I remember one session when John Kane challenged the truth of my statement and I put my hand on Bob Brown's shoulder and said to John. "If I'm not telling the truth, I'll set Bob on fire here and now!" I made my point and Bob continues to remind me of that incident.

Registration. Unfortunately, my childhood acquaintance turned out to be a problem drinker...both off the job and on and was often in trouble at work because of his drinking.

Industry in general and the nuclear industry took a dim view of on-the-job effects of alcohol and drugs. It was inevitable that his drinking would catch up with him. He was caught in several situations and subjected to disciplinary measures. Termination of employment seemed inevitable based on the 'three strike' principle.

One of the most egregious incidents involved a night shift and his taking of hourly readings of the level of liquid in a large storage tank. Somehow, the tank contracted a serious leak. Undaunted, this childhood acquaintance of mine waded through ankle-deep liquid in a containment well and, undaunted by sloshing through the leaking contents of the tank, he took his readings.

He continued throughout the night dutifully recording the rapidly diminishing tank level every hour on the hour as required. He made no comment on the growing volume of liquid in the well nor the rapidly falling level of the tank. He raised no alarm nor take any action; he just took readings. By morning of the next day, the tank was empty.

## CAPE BRETON FRIENDS

### A Rollie MacInnis Story

I grew up in Cape Breton where I went to school, played sports and made friends. When I joined the Glace Bay plant in 1977 I discovered that there was a dozen or more people on the payroll with whom I had some prior connection. Some were school friends, others were friends I made during my many years of playing hockey, baseball, fastball. Still others were people with direct or indirect family connections to me or my family. Recently, one of my friends asked me how these renewed relationships affected me and my job. With rare exceptions, there was no solicitation of employment or other favours. There was only one incident where I was obliged to impose a disciplinary penalty on a Cape Breton acquaintance. I did receive a few phone calls however, one from a grandmother, one from a priest, asking for my assistance in offering summer employment to a deserving student of limited means. For the most part my relationships were a very positive factor. Occasionally I had the opportunity to share a memory with one or more employees but, for the most part, we just did our jobs and separated our work and private lives. I think we all knew how to behave.

# ROLLIE POEMS

## ODE TO HEAVY WATER

*A Poem*
*by*
*Rollie MacInnis*
*Written in 1973*

Elusive liquid
We've been told
You're hard to get
And hard to hold

Your extra neutron
Gives you weight
Perhaps that's why
You're always late

At DCL you slipped of the noose
And cook a big fat Tory goose
They've cornered you at CGE
But not in any quantity
Now you lie in wait at Bruce
Our H2S will turn you loose
It's all out war, we'll shoot to kill
And boil your body in our still.

## THE ROOM BENEATH THE STAIRS

Or¶

Everything you wanted to know about space allocation but were afraid to

ask!

*A poem by*
*Rollie MacInnis*


I visited CGE, I did,
and guess what I saw there
a bunch of inspectors doing their thing
in a room beneath the stairs
I said to myself, "that's not for me",
it certainly seems unfair
to ask a group to do their thing
in a room beneath the stairs

It was crowded and cramped and dungeon – like
with no view of the open air
but they cheerfully did the best they could
from the room beneath the stairs

and so, to us in our own little plant
with all of the planning and care
shortly is likely we won't be kept in the room beneath the stairs
I've studied the plans and I conclude
our chances are less than fair that we shall have the luxury of
a room beneath the stairs

*Written by Roland MacInnis in April 1971 at BHWP*


NOTE: In 1970, the inspection team at the CGE plant in Port
Hawkesbury was housed in a small space in a room beneath a stairway. As
a newly hired Materials and Inspection Supervisor for the Bruce Heavy

Water Plant, I was assigned to the CGE plant prior to a reassignment to the Savannah River plant in South Carolina. Upon arrival at Bruce I was offered a small space in the Maintenance Building for the M&I team and I turned it down. The Materials and Inspection team lived in a temporary construction warehouse until new facilities were constructed. It seems that the plant architects woefully underestimated the Production and Maintenance facilities required for an 800-ton Heavy Water Plant. - Rollie MacInnis

# APPENDIX 2

## HEAVY WATER

Heavy water looks, feels, and tastes like ordinary water. It occurs naturally. About 1 part in 7000 in any amount of naturally occurring water, including drinking water, is heavy water. It's pretty much like your everyday water, it's just heavier. Although it's often associated with atomic energy, in its natural state, it is not radioactive.

Without belabouring the science too much, you might remember from school that every molecule of water has two atoms of hydrogen and one atom of oxygen, the chemical symbol is, [H2O].

Heavy water is heavier because the hydrogen is a special kind of hydrogen, an isotope, called 'deuterium'.

It's still hydrogen, just…well…heavier.

Deuterium is twice as heavy as ordinary hydrogen and, I won't do the math… trust me… heavy water is 10% heavier.

Ten percent! Big deal! As it turns out, it is a big deal.

In the early days of atomic research, it was discovered that heavy water could slow down or 'moderate' neutrons and thus help to produce an atomic chain reaction in radioactive uranium…where atoms split, and neutrons fly off to split even more atoms in a wild atomic dance that generates heat.

I'm not talking explosions, atomic bombs or the like. I'm talking about generating heat in a nuclear reactor. Creating heat and producing steam, whether by oil, gas, coal, or uranium is the backbone of today's electrical system.

There are other ways to generate electricity but that is beyond the scope of this book. There are also other uses for heavy water and uranium beyond peaceful atomic power and that too is beyond the scope of this book.

I'll conclude this short explanatory chapter by saying that Canada invented its own type of nuclear reactor called a CANDU reactor which needs approximately a ton of heavy water for every million watts of electrical power capacity. Heavy water isn't consumed in the process and so, except for losses due to leaks, once a CANDU reactor is filled with heavy water, it only needs to be 'topped up' or 'cleaned up' every now and then.

## IS HEAVY WATER DANGEROUS?

The short answer, insofar as humans are concerned, is, 'not particularly'. Accidental or intentional poisoning is unlikely given the large quantities that would have to be ingested to produce harmful effects in humans.

Having said that you wouldn't want to taste it, drink it or otherwise play with it. The Canadian Nuclear Safety Commission (CNSC) regulates possession, use, packaging, transport, storage, and import and export of heavy water to protect the health, safety and security of Canadians. Furthermore, at about C$1000 a kg, it's too valuable.

## HYDROGEN SULPHIDE – H2S

Hydrogen sulphide gas is extremely toxic. It is, by any definition, a poison.

Many people are familiar with the smell of boiled eggs. However, you cannot rely on your sense of smell to detect H2S. What is important is knowing that breathing 300 parts per million or more of hydrogen sulphide gas can prove fatal.

A rule of thumb in the heavy water industry is that the amount of hydrogen sulphide in a plant approximates its production capacity. Thus, heavy water plants contain hundreds of tons of 100% hydrogen sulphide gas. The Armageddon scenario for a heavy water plant is the leakage and spread of hundreds of tons of deadly gas, caused by a major rupture in a pipe or vessel. Hydrogen sulphide, when mixed with air in just the right amount, is highly explosive. If, upon its initial release, the gas-air mixture encounters an initiating spark, the resulting explosion would be equivalent to an explosion of many hundred tons of TNT.

Heavy water plants using the GS process, like Glace Bay, have very rigorous safety programs. These programs are designed to protect employees and people in surrounding communities. Heavy water production at GBHWP was governed by the Atomic Energy Control Act. This meant that the plant could only operate under a license issued by the Atomic Energy Control Board, the administrators of the act.

One of the most important conditions of the operating license was the Emergency Plan. This plan required notification the surrounding community in the event of a release of toxic gas. The plan enlisted the aid of police, fire, medical and civil authorities. The plant practised implementation of the emergency plan regularly. Fortunately, it was never put it into effect.

The first principle in safety, is to "know the hazard." In heavy water plants this meant that employees at all levels are required to know about the hazards of hydrogen sulphide and the best means of protection under any circumstances.

Employees who worked in the process areas of the plant were required to train regularly and rigorously. This included knowledge and use of personal safety equipment, such as protective breathing apparatus, and how to render assistance to another person in the event of H2S poisoning.

For example, in monthly training sessions employees were required to demonstrate their ability to use their own protective breathing equipment, sound a plant wide alarm, assemble and wear self-contained breathing apparatus, and use a "buddy mask" to rescue an incapacitated person. Realistic 'dummy' models were used for this demonstration. Records were kept of these sessions and were a requirement of our operating license.

Each morning the emergency signals were tested, the alert, the emergency, and the all clear. Regular rescue drills were held by production shifts where they demonstrated their ability to rescue a person who, for example, might be 100 feet high on an access platform. The plant owned and operated an ambulance and a fire truck with fully trained crews on the 24 x 7 basis.

A fully equipped medical clinic was also on site with a full-time day time nurse, Bev Macintosh, and each shift had first aid trained personnel. The plant also had, under contract, a medical doctor who made regular visits to our clinic to determine employee health status.

A Plant Safety Manual to ensured that employees had good information on known hazards and were trained in what to do should an accident, or incident occur.

## THE GS PROCESS

GS stands for Girdler-Sulphide. This process was used by the USAEC at its various plants in the USA. For example, the Savannah River Plant located on a huge 'reservation' bordering the Savannah River in South Carolina.

Deuterium can be captured from ordinary water by cascading it through successive hot and cold vessels, [towers] at high pressure.

Here is a rhyme that captures this idea: *'Deuterium will pass from the liquid to gas if the tower is hot…otherwise it will not.'*

Thus, deuterium concentrates in the gas in the hot tower and in the liquid in the cold tower. By moving gas and liquid forward in successive steps, through hot and cold towers, deuterium may be concentrated to about 20% and then it can be upgraded to 99.75% using an ordinary distillation process. This is an oversimplification. There are many aspects of heavy water physics and chemistry that require sophisticated chemical engineering skill if one is to design, build and operate a heavy water plant.


## END

www.ingramcontent.com/pod-product-compliance
Lightning Source LLC
Chambersburg PA
CBHW051317220526
45468CB00004B/1381